Storytelling for New Technologies and Platforms

Want to know what it's like to write for a theme park attraction? Or an interactive toy? Or a virtual reality game? *Wait – those tell stories? And there are jobs for people who write them?* Thanks to technology, interactive products and live experiences can now engage us with memorable characters and exciting adventures that were once destined only for the cinema.

Storytelling for New Technologies and Platforms: A Writer's Guide to Theme Parks, Virtual Reality, Board Games, Virtual Assistants, and More is a handbook for writers, students, producers, teachers, scholars, career changers, early tech adopters, and just about anyone who loves story and technology. As a collection of articles from some of the best creative writers in their medium, this book will prepare content creators of tomorrow to tackle some of today's most exhilarating creative challenges found on a screen... or off!

Key features:

- Expert advice from several industry professionals who have worked for some of the world's biggest tech and interactive companies.

- Best practices that not only guide writers on how to apply their craft to new fields but also prepare them for the common ambiguity they will find in corporate and start-up environments.

- Breakdown of platforms that shows how tech capabilities can fulfill content expectations and how content can fulfill tech expectations.

- Basic storytelling mechanics customized to today's popular technologies, live experiences, and traditional game platforms.

Storytelling for New Technologies and Platforms

A Writer's Guide to Theme Parks, Virtual Reality, Board Games, Virtual Assistants, and More

Edited by

Ross Berger

CRC Press
Taylor & Francis Group
Boca Raton London New York

CRC Press is an imprint of the
Taylor & Francis Group, an **informa** business

First edition published 2022
by CRC Press
6000 Broken Sound Parkway NW, Suite 300, Boca Raton, FL 33487-2742

and by CRC Press
4 Park Square, Milton Park, Abingdon, Oxon, OX14 4RN

CRC Press is an imprint of Taylor & Francis Group, LLC

Library of Congress Cataloging-in-Publication Data
Names: Berger, Ross, editor.
Title: Storytelling for new technologies and platforms : a writer's guide
to theme parks, virtual reality, board games, virtual assistants, and
more / edited by Ross Berger.
Description: First edition. | Boca Raton : CRC Press 2022. |
Includes bibliographical references and index. | Summary: "This is a practical
guide for writers, students, producers, career changers, and early tech
adopters. It will prepare the content creators of tomorrow with the best
practices of storytelling for virtual assistants, virtual reality,
mobile games, board games, hybrid games, interactive toys, and theme
park attractions"—Provided by publisher.
Identifiers: LCCN 2021059848 | ISBN 9780367693831 (hardback) |
ISBN 9780367693787 (paperback) | ISBN 9781003141594 (ebook)
Subjects: LCSH: Video games—Authorship. | Storytelling. | Virtual reality.|
Games and technology. | Video games—Design.
Classification: LCC GV1469.34.A97 S76 2022 | DDC 794.8/1535—dc23
LC record available at https://lccn.loc.gov/2021059848

ISBN: 9780367693831 (hbk)
ISBN: 9780367693787 (pbk)
ISBN: 9781003141594 (ebk)

DOI: 10.1201/9781003141594

Typeset in Minion
by codeMantra

Contents

Preface: Why This Book

IN THE PAST, MANY high-tech companies – both start-up and established – approached me to help them craft a story universe for a new consumer technology that promised to change the world. These new technologies were not improvements of current products, but actual new product categories. The technology in question wasn't a video game, as I was accustomed to doing. But because I had worked in that industry, that is, because I had worked with engineers, I was well suited to take on a new challenge in an adjacent field. My work for these high-tech clients took me to worlds inside a virtual reality headset, to television shows that could change storylines instantly with the tap of a finger on a screen, to a robot that helped kids on the spectrum understand the world around them.

These weren't just jobs, but adventures. For me, experiencing new technologies is as exciting as exploring a country I've never been to before. In my work, I feel empowered when traversing uncharted territory, creating a storytelling grammar from which others could evolve.

Not long after these experiences, I discovered that I was not alone. I met other writers who chartered similar terrain but for competing products. And then I met others who dwelled in adjacent worlds, creating story experiences for amusement park rides, digital board games, and virtual assistants. We got to talking (at a high level, mind you) about tackling new content challenges on untested technologies. There were shared methods, synergies, and many lessons to learn. After the wonderful experience I had codifying my best practices for video games in the book *Dramatic Storytelling & Narrative Design: A Writer's Guide to Video Games and Transmedia* (CRC Press, 2020), I thought it best to do a follow-up for storytelling for new technologies and platforms, but to seek out the contributions from colleagues whose unique experiences and points of view would add unique depth and meaningful variety from which readers, students, and writers-to-be would benefit heavily.

This book is a collection of those points of view, articles written by some of the best creative writers in technology today. I am humbled by their participation and awed by their insight.

Yet, as new technologies continue to proliferate our homes, there isn't a single event or product that motivated the writing of this book. However, by the fact that I am meeting more people every day who undertake new technology content assignments indicates that there is progress afoot, significant enough where billions of dollars from the world's biggest companies are funneling toward disruptive technologies as I write this.

It's a very exciting time to be a storyteller. There are more avenues than ever before, and worlds once thought impossible to create or too fantastical to build are now in countless homes across the world.

WHY THESE CONTRIBUTORS WERE CHOSEN

The contributors of this volume were chosen specifically for their creative writing prowess in their respective medium. They are tough critics of their own work; that's what makes them exceptional. They are also tough critics of media in general, and are forthright and eloquent when an experience doesn't meet their bar of excellence.

Their articles contain gems of wisdom, precious in their unique perspective. Their words are considerate; at times, raw; always instructive. They will not be selling readers snake oil. When a project works, their views are communicated from a deep place of experience and passion. When a project doesn't work, they come from a place of humility and expertise. These writers never think their field is better than others'. They, in fact, love to tell stories and experience stories as much as anyone else. They have no agenda other than to tell the best story possible. And for this book, their goals are the same: to share their points of view of what works best in their chosen field. They instruct through experience; they lead through experience.

WHO THIS BOOK IS MEANT FOR

This book is aimed toward students, professionals, writers who are exploring something new, and just about anyone who didn't know that amusement parks or toys or board games can tell stories. The firsthand perspective of practicing writers in the field offers critical knowledge that cannot be taught in the classroom by creative tourists. Their words are primers to real world experience, but more so are entry points into unchartered frontiers of the growing storytelling landscape.

Yesterday, this landscape included books, radio, film, television. Today, it includes video games, interactive television shows, board games, mobile games, interactive toys, virtual assistants, virtual reality, augmented reality, A.I., amusement park rides. Tomorrow? To wherever new technologies evolve, you can guarantee that its early days will involve stories, games, spectacle, habit-forming activities, and all of the above.

To learn how to solve for the creative challenges that these technologies present is to equip the storytellers of tomorrow with the necessary tools for success. It is my hope that this book instills within them the confidence to take on the unknown, the impossible.

FRIENDLY DISCLAIMER

This book is not an academic exploration that analyzes the effectiveness of different story methodologies found in new technologies. Rather, it is a book primarily about best practices from highly sought-after writing professionals who have worked for years in industry on emerging technologies and platforms. Their points of view are often anecdotal but authoritative, analytical but not impersonal. For the vast majority, these contributors have written for numerous media (mostly interactive) for some of the world's biggest tech companies or high-value entertainment products. Most of these writers, individually, have more than a decade's worth of experience and are now sharing their industry insight and best practices for the first time.

Traditional video games, as a storytelling medium, serve as foundational knowledge for most, if not all, of these chapters. This is no mistake, for technology that endeavors to tell stories often looks to games as a model. To be clear: video games are high technology and, for decades, they've paved the way for VR, robots, theme parks, and other innovations that combine tech and content.

TERMINOLOGY

In this book, you'll find countless references to "platform." I (and many of my fellow contributors) will use it interchangeably with terms like "medium," "new technology," or "ecosystem." Basically, a platform is a showcase of media or content.[1] For example, a stage is a platform that showcases numerous plays within a single year. In the high-tech world, a company's platform is proprietary with its own brandable design and unique capabilities.

---

[1] Media or content qualifies as music, games, information (audio or visual), story, learning programs, health tracking, social media, art, performance, etc.

The Netflix streaming service, for example, is a visually distinct platform, with a very identifiable user interface, with a seamless, no lag streaming of countless films or TV shows that can be accessed on different devices from different tech companies. In technology, identifying the showcase (and hence, platform) can be a tricky thing as one tends to think of hardware first, like the Kindle Fire e-reader or the Xbox gaming console. "Showcase" ought not refer to the hardware necessarily, or rather not exclusively to hardware. Take, for example, Apple's iOS. Its platform is the computing operating system for its mobile devices like the iPhone or the iPad – and only for Apple hardware (unlike Google's Android mobile operating system, which can be accessed on non-Google hardware). Hence, an app created exclusively for the iOS platform can be accessed on both Apple's iPhone and iPad hardware (and sometimes on its computers). But in the rare case where a closed operating system appears on a singular hardware (such as the short-lived robot Jibo), both the operating system and the singular hardware qualify as the platform. Platform also refers to smaller showcases that are singular experiences like board games and amusement park rides (platform that is the ride itself, not the amusement park). More commonly, these are referred to as "experiences," but this book will refer to these as platforms as well.

"Storytellers" and "storytelling" are used too frequently today to a point of meaninglessness. Marketing campaigns, TED Talks, self-help gurus, and corporate communications experts use this term to add more heft and emotional investment to the work that they do. However, "storytelling" really isn't devoted to creating an ephemeral mood or a framework for understanding one's purpose in life. It is a fictional journey following a hero who undergoes highs and lows which culminate in the loss or gain of high-value consequences, whereupon the hero achieves self-discovery. "Storytelling" is another way of saying "drama" or "fiction." And those who create stories – aka "storytellers" – are also known as "writers," "creative writers," "dramatists," "screenwriters," "authors," "content designers," "content creators" (equally as overused), or "narrative designers."

Lastly, the target of storytelling, the *raison d'etre* of our presence in the tech and entertainment industry, is the consumer. This is not to be confused with the purchaser of product (though, that is implied); rather, it is the individual that consumes media. The consumer is synonymous with "user," "end user," "audience" (likely referring to more than one consumer and in reference to film and television), "player" or "gamer" (in reference to video games and interactive entertainment), and "customer."

Ross Berger

Acknowledgments

SPECIAL THANKS TO BAY Anapol, Rob Auten, Sarah Beaulieu, Flint Dille, Zane Dille, James Laks, Matt Parker, and Maurice Suckling. To Rick Adams, who made this book possible, and to Randi Cohen and Will Bateman, who shepherded its publication. Also deserving of recognition are Josh Feldman and Jan Libby, whose discussions in person and/or over email proved invaluable. To my dog, Lacey: I thank you for our morning walks and your adorable snoring. To Liat, my *motek*: I love you.

Lastly, during the final weeks before submission of this book to CRC Press, I lost my dear uncle, Selman "Sandy" Berger. A retired chemistry professor, Sandy was an endless source of encouragement when it came to exploring my craft in publishing and academia. I will miss him dearly, and I dedicate this book to him.

Ross Berger

Editor

Ross Berger is a writer, narrative designer, and transmedia strategist based in Los Angeles. He is the author of *Dramatic Storytelling & Narrative Design: A Writer's Guide to Video Games & Transmedia* (CRC Press, 2020), a "how to" for fledgling game writers and screenwriters. His screenwriting credits include *Law & Order* and the Webby-Award winning *LonelyGirl15*. He also served as the supervising producer for the social media/television experience *The Runner*. Ross has also worked extensively in virtual reality as a writer for the Oculus Rift launch title *Farlands* and the award-winning thriller *Eclipse: Edge of Light* for the Google Daydream and Oculus Go. As a narrative designer in the video game industry, he has written AAA games for Microsoft, Electronic Arts, and many others. Ross is also the author of short stories including "Football with Leatherman" (2020) and "Evie A.I." (2021), both published by TulipTree Publishing in its *Stories That Need to Be Told* anthologies.

A graduate of Brandeis (BA, Philosophy) and Columbia (MFA, Playwriting) universities, Ross is a member of the Writers Guild of America and the Television Academy.

Contributors

Bay Anapol received her MFA in Creative Writing from the University of Arkansas, later attending Stanford University as a Stegner Fellow in Fiction. Her work has been published in the *Laurel Review, Story Magazine, Michigan Quarterly Review, Gulf Coast, Manoa,* and the *2001 Pushcart Prize Collection.* She has worked in game narrative design for over a decade, designing and writing everything from Microsoft's *Project Spark* to numerous casual titles like *Gummy Drop!* and *Decurse.* Since 2019, she has been the narrative director at FunPlus.

Rob Auten is the co-founder of Hexagram, an interactive production studio whose clients and partners include Hollywood studios, theme parks, and some of the world's biggest technology companies. Prior to founding Hexagram, he held creative leadership positions on billion-dollar video game franchises including *Gears of War* and *Battlefield.* His work has been awarded with a Games BAFTA and twice nominated for interactive Emmy awards. He is a Sundance New Frontier Lab fellow and has been granted several patents for his work in Augmented and Virtual Reality.

After years of writing plays and short films, doctoring scripts, and teaching screenwriting, **Sarah Beaulieu** entered the world of interactive fiction. Since then, she has worked on several video game and VR productions as a writer and narrative designer. She recently wrote for *Beyond Good & Evil 2* (Ubisoft), before starting as an associate narrative director on the *Assassin's Creed* franchise. Sarah loves discovering new ways of telling stories and learning the art of fiction from every possible field. Today, she keeps writing and building fictional worlds for multiple media, with a particular affection for science-fiction, fantasy, and historical stories.

Flint Dille started his career by turning toys into TV shows with G1 *Transformers* (and the movie), *G.I. Joe*, *Inhumanoids*, and *Visionaries*. He has designed games with Gary Gygax and written movies for Steven Spielberg. Flint has sold game design documents as feature films twice – *Venom* (Dimension, 2006) and *Agent in Place* (Lionsgate, 2010). Flint's lore book for the video game *Diablo III: Book of Cain* charted on the New York Times Best Sellers List, and his digital *Transformers* comic *Autocracy* was 2012's best-selling digital-only comic. Flint has twice won "Game Script of the Year" for *Riddick: Escape from Butcher Bay* (with JZP) and *Dead to Rights*, and was nominated for *Ghostbusters* and *Dark Athena*. Recently, Flint was Creative Lead at Niantic Labs (makers of *Ingress* and *Pokémon GO*) from 2012 to 2020. In July 2020, his memoir, *The Gamesmaster: My Life in the '80s Geek Culture Trenches with G.I. Joe, Dungeons & Dragons, and The Transformers*, was released.

Zane Dille is a research analyst and writer situated at the intersection of technological and humanistic inquiry. His most recent project is Polyplexus, a platform that harnesses game and social practices to create better scientific research proposals for DARPA. He graduated from the University of Southern California with bachelor's degrees in philosophy and classics.

James "Jamie" Laks is an analog game designer based in Troy, NY. A graduate of Rensselaer Polytechnic Institute's program for Games and Simulation Arts and Sciences in 2020, James is currently a member of the Institute's inaugural cohort of their PhD program in Critical Game Design. His digital research focuses primarily on experimental narrative design and cross-media storytelling, combining the interactive aspects of games with other forms of narrative, like television and film. James is the Gold Award winner for the "Game Narrative Review" competition at the 2018 Game Developers Conference.

Matt Parker has led the creative direction for a variety of award-winning shows, attractions, and exhibitions for some of popular culture's most beloved properties, including *Harry Potter*, *Looney Tunes*, and DC Comics. What began as an early fascination (though some might say obsession) with theme parks, theater, and film later evolved into an incredible career in an industry that continues to grow. Matt is a graduate of the University of Southern California.

Maurice Suckling is an award-winning game developer who has contributed to over 50 published video games, including *Fortnite* and *Borderlands: The Pre-Sequel*. He is the co-writer of *Video Game Writing: From Macro to Micro*. He is the designer of several board games, including *Freeman's Farm: 1777*, *Chancellorsville: 1863*, *Hidden Strike: American Revolution*, and *Siege of Malta: 1565*. Outside of games he works in film (*The Devil Only Walks* – in pre-production), TV (*Alphablocks* – BBC TV), and fiction (*Photocopies of Heaven*). He is an assistant professor in the Games and Simulation Arts and Sciences Program and the Communication and Media Department at Rensselaer Polytechnic Institute in Troy, New York. His major research interests are innovation in game stories and analog historical simulations. He holds a PhD in Creative Writing from Newcastle University, a Master's in global history from the University of Birmingham, and a Bachelor of Arts in Religion with Literature from the University of Bristol.

How This Book Is Organized

CONTENTS

O NE CAN READ THE articles in this book separately from one another, that is, a contributor didn't write their article conditionally or symbiotically to the work of another's. In aggregate, the articles carry similar themes, similar insights, and (sometimes) similar best practices. Nonetheless, each one's order of appearance reflects a deliberate calculus.

Upon final review of each contribution, I observed two common denominators that persisted as secondary or subtle requirements of each writer's chosen platform: **location** (where to experience the storytelling platform) and **social nature** (with whom to experience the storytelling platform). While these might seem like obvious criteria for product designers or game designers, they are not so obvious for storytellers. So subtle are these requirements that I dare say these are not the prime focus – or not one of the most prime foci – when a writer applies their craft to a nontraditional storytelling platform. They might be innate considerations, but seldom are they drivers of story.

However, *where* the platform is experienced and *with whom* are, together, design criteria that, consciously or not, impact the overall user experience greatly. And since designers, technologists, and storytellers follow the user experience, or rather create for the end user (as opposed to themselves or

DOI: 10.1201/9781003141594-1

a groupthink cohort), the "location/social nature" model demands attention. Be they the prime focus or the necessary criteria, location and social nature are defining characteristics of new storytelling platforms, and as such, impact the ways stories are told.

Let it be known that this "location/social nature" model doesn't have to be the lens through which the reader views these ensuing articles. It is my lens, however, and if this framework happens to catch on in academic circles, then hallelujah. If not, then you can deem the rest of this introduction as ramblings and skip ahead to the next contributor. Otherwise, bear with me as I attempt to explain this model's impact on new storytelling platforms of today.

LOCATION: SHARED VS. EXCLUSIVE

The platforms described in this book require a user to be in either a shared space or an exclusive space. A **shared space** includes arcades, amusement parks, concerts, theaters, or even the street. I refer to it as "shared" because consumers are likely to be in the same space, experiencing the same ride, live experience, installation, etc. with others. (Keep in mind, however, that does not mean the platform assumes the people are multifarious; it could very well speak to the body of people as if they were one individual. More about this later.)

The goal here is to interact with the platform in a way that is either reliant upon a spectacle that cannot be experienced in a home or is so unique to its native environment that it requires people to witness it there and only there. Other examples include haunted houses and simulated period pieces (e.g., Renaissance Fair, historical reenactments).

An **exclusive space** – the most popular kind – refers to a single locale, often limited in scope and capability. A consumer's home qualifies most obviously. It could also include one's car or office. The notion of privacy or limited involvement from others is the defining trait of the exclusive space. It is in the exclusive space where one feels most secure, where they will interact with a technology or platform more regularly upon their own pace and schedule, and/or interact with others as well. One's home might be limited in set design and spectacle, but that's not how one chooses to have fun at home. Experiences are designed to take advantage of one's limited space by providing ongoing or episodic entertainment or replayable experiences so that the consumer is motivated to engage with that platform continually. On the other hand, shared space events are self-contained experiences, primarily one-offs, that play up the spectacle of the environment because typical consumers will not have access to that environment (and the moment in time in which it is to be engaged) regularly or ever again.

SOCIAL NATURE: INTERDEPENDENT VS. AUTONOMOUS

Most products, be they tangible or digital, involve a singularly minded engagement between consumer and product. That is, the design and purpose of the product is to fulfill a specific need for one person at a given time – for example, pressing a bottle for a dollop of shampoo or using a fork to deliver a morsel of food to one's mouth. Granted, consumers can undermine the intention of the product to have multiple people experience said product at a given time. Any product or service is elastic when "hacked." But the intention of design for most consumer products is overwhelmingly single consumer focused.

That said, today's interactive consumer products have evolved from that mindset and are no longer single-focused only. This, we can attribute to the traditional "online" computer and – since 2007 with the advent of the smartphone – to mobile carriers and Wi-Fi. A gaming experience over the phone, for example, could be designed to be played by more than one person at a given time and, as such, falls apart if it's played singularly. Therefore, it's important to distinguish if the interactive platforms of today are either **interdependent** or **autonomous** *by intention*. The social status greatly shifts consumer expectations and, accordingly, how the product is designed and how a story is told through it.

Interdependent experiences, in short, are designed to be experienced by multiple participants and cannot be experienced without more than one person. The content and activities assume that there are multiple people engaging in the experience concurrently. On the other hand, an autonomous experience comprises content and activities for one entity in mind.

Another salient point: an interdependent experience requires that its participants (be they live competitors or live allies) move it forward. In other words, in absence of their participation, the experience would stall. Not surprisingly, a single entity (be it a group or individual – more about this in the "Shared + Autonomous" section) must also participate in order to move the autonomous experience forward. This single entity, however, does not need a live opposing force, competitor, or helper to do so. But the autonomous experience does require, at least, bare minimum self-governing participation (e.g., taking one's seat on a *Harry Potter* ride) to activate or validate it.

Now, there are autonomous experiences that are enhanced by the presence of others. *Pokémon GO*, the mobile augmented reality hit that was launched in 2016, was originally designed for the singular experience, where a player collects rare and popular digital Pokémon characters through their phone that translates the open, real world into a digital landscape. *Pokémon GO* rapidly became a social phenomenon where people joined live, physical groups to wander the free world and discover Pokémon together. While social in the physical world, the interactivity on the screen remained autonomous, as collecting Pokémon was agnostic to the number of participants and/or who was by a player's side. Then came the Raids and the Gyms, where the interdependent experience took over. Players were assigned a team to fight (digitally and together) for rare Pokémon. Both experiences still exist for *Pokémon GO*, though the Raids and Gyms have gone through periodic design upgrades.

Pokémon GO proves that there are, of course, exceptions to the rule and that there are hybrid experiences. But these experiences evolve to become exceptions and hybrids in order to tend to a rising customer need. Seldom do they enter the marketplace that way.

EXCLUSIVE + AUTONOMOUS

Experiences that involve an exclusive space for the autonomous consumer require a dedicated space for said consumer, where the area of usage need not require change or the presence of a tangible totem except for the interactive platform itself. This is an experience that is designed for the singular consumer. Such experiences include the virtual assistant platform (e.g., Siri, Alexa, Google Home); interactive toys (e.g., Tamagotchi, Disney's Playmation action figures); video games; virtual reality; and mobile games.

The latter three straddle the line between "Exclusive" and "Shared" as well as "Autonomous" and "Interdependent"; however, most experiences created for the mobile, console, and VR platforms qualify as exclusive and autonomous when story is involved. Writing additional, various stories wholesale for multiple players is often unrealistic for a development team in mobile, console, and VR (typically due to budget and personnel limitations); as such, most of the storytelling in these platforms remain single consumer focused. Although line variations are common when players can choose different characters as avatars in a video game, a player shouldn't expect meaningful plot changes, as they are too costly to pull off and quality assure.

Chapters grouped under "Exclusive + Autonomous" include:

Flint Dille and Zane Dille's "Virtual Assistants and Storytelling"

Rob Auten's "Writing for Toys – Actually a Job"

Sarah Beaulieu's "Approaching Virtual Reality Storytelling"

Bay Anapol's "Building Narrative in Mobile Games"

EXCLUSIVE + INTERDEPENDENT

Platforms that require the consumer's exclusive environment but can only be experienced with multiple participants include board games; video games; mobile games; virtual reality; and interactive toys. (The latter four straddle the line, once again, but will qualify as Exclusive + Autonomous when, as explained in the previous section, story is involved.)

Board games – be they luddite or digital hybrids – offer a unique storytelling experience mainly because the board game experience cannot progress without the participation of more than one person. So, whether it's a turned-based or time-keeping system, the revelation or evolution of story cannot move forward without the collaboration or opposition of other live players. That said, some digital hybrids offer the autonomous experience as an addition to (or substitution of) the interdependent experience, but the intention of the product is to be experienced by more than one person at a single time. Autonomy, in these games, may be a design pillar, but it is not the ideal vision of how the product was conceived or even marketed. That's why these games offer (and recommend) playability of up to four or five people.

Side note: video games, like some hybrid board games, often offer single and cooperative modes, allowing players to choose to play by themselves or with others. But the number of participants has no bearing on the story once the mode is chosen. While there can be variations in dialogue to accommodate the additional player(s), the storyline (if there is one) for that mode remains the same.

Chapters grouped under "Exclusive + Interdependent" include:

Maurice Suckling's "Storytelling and Board Games"

James Laks's "Storytelling in Hybrid Games"

SHARED + AUTONOMOUS

It almost seems oxymoronic to experience a game or activity autonomously in a shared locale. Does one not come across others in this experience? Or wouldn't the presence of others influence how the experience is engaged?

Not necessarily. An amusement park ride is in a shared space, shared often with family and strangers, dozens at a time. The story – often a brief mission that is completed within the duration of the ride – does not typically involve branching narrative or customized or differentiated content.

It is a uniform experience for all, whose primary fun derives from locomotion and/or visual spectacle. Story grounds the experience in context or details that expand a beloved, established franchise (e.g., the rides of *Harry Potter and the Forbidden Journey* and *Star Wars Millennium Falcon*). Story is a bit of a stretch here, as the audience is pursuing a mission, simulated of course, short-term but adrenaline-fueled. Nonetheless, what happens in that quicksilver experience requires a series of escalating events that comes from the imagination of a writer (or creative director fulfilling the role of a writer).

Yet, the story of each ride does not change based on the number of participants. The simulation is intense but is not sensitive or nimble. In other words, if either one person or one hundred people participate at the same time within the same space, the story does not change. It is, therefore, an autonomous experience because the story and interactivity are fixed and engageable by one entity. That is, the ride pursues its fixed path without any distinction between a *single individual* and a *single group* of individuals.

The chapter grouped under "Shared + Autonomous" include:

Matt Parker's "The Shape of Story"

SHARED + INTERDEPENDENT

These experiences are often loose versions of the "Shared + Autonomous" model. ARGs (alternate reality games) and augmented reality ("AR") experiences are often focused on one thing: a goal-oriented activity, be it the acquiring of an item, the discovering of a location, or the solving of a puzzle. One who participates in this must collaborate with others, taking on a shared role with another but as part of a unified front. Or, those participants are divided based on specialties and roles (e.g., the codebreaker, the fast runner, the organizer, etc.).

Escape rooms are the best example of this today. They offer fun and suspenseful morale-building activities. They challenge people – be they friends, co-workers, or strangers – to work together under tremendous stress to solve a series of challenges that culminates with the escape from the facility or domicile. Now, while it is expected that a group will participate in a single experience, the solving of challenges to escape a room are not uniquely or rigidly interdependent. Yes, multiple tasks might confront a team at certain levels, but that's an uncreative extension of the singular task of answering logic puzzles or breaking codes or rummaging a landscape for physical clues or keys. A single person could accomplish these tasks alone and experience the same content and results as groups do.

The storytelling tropes for this are mundane. Because the Shared + Interdependent experience is so task-driven, story is delivered through chunks after the completion of said task. "Story" here (if you can call it that) is basically a thin justification for why tasks need to be accomplished. Save the damsel in distress before it's too late. Capture the bad guy before he gets away or kills your team. Et cetera, et cetera.

The real story is the real-life interpersonal experiences players have with one another. Do they enjoy the collaboration with others? Are they making new friends? This is the true magic behind the Shared + Interdependent experience. But these are emergent experiences – emotional byproducts and reactions, not a scripted journey.

So, is there a pure Shared + Interdependent story experience? Not that I've encountered and, hence, why there isn't a chapter devoted to this combination. There is potential though in an experience where multiple players must make simultaneous decisions, not as a game show gimmick, but as an organic driver of story.

Consider a high stakes war simulation in a *Jason Bourne*-esque command center, where ten players must scour intelligence reports individually (e.g., satellite imagery, aerial footage, open-source social media intelligence, human intelligence), build a thesis upon limited information, and work together to achieve consensus when executing a single decision (e.g., deployment of troops, initiation of air strikes, launching a cyber-attack, etc.) that (hopefully) leads to military progression and enemy neutralization until mission accomplished. More specifically: A computerized data center (nothing more complex than an online hub) doles out the mission and the intelligence reports. Each player has the same amount of time to solve their part of the intelligence mosaic before unifying it with others. Players then discuss and debate until they reach a unanimous consensus. Once the team enters their military decision, the computer replies with a right or wrong answer and the respective consequences: a wrong decision leads to lives lost, enemy advancement, and expulsion of players; a right decision leads to gradual advancement of your military; constant debate leads to no decision, enemy advancement, and an expulsion of players. The computer doles out the next part of the mission and its respective intelligence reports. The process continues.

The storytelling here is simple: advance into enemy territory until you vanquish the opposition with force… or until they vanquish you first. The narrative highs and lows will depend upon the success of your collaboration with others and the skills you have at interpreting clues. The collaborative moments are not scripted events, however, even though they promise to be the most exciting part of the entire experience. The narrative richness within each intelligence report serves as a unique opportunity for the creative writer to shine. Here, the world is story: what is the terrain of this land; who are its people; how do they respond to your mistakes; what is the emotional impact of making a right decision vs. a wrong one.

STORYTELLING FACTOR

As mentioned earlier, many of the platforms tackled in this book straddle the line between shared and exclusive, interdependent and autonomous. But when storytelling is added into the mix, the straddling diminishes. Why storytelling impacts the location/social nature criteria is a testament to the intention of the experience and the reality of building it.

Regarding the latter, most interactive entertainment experiences do not prioritize story. Technology, art, sound, user experience design… elements that are visually stunning, fun to play, cinematic to listen to often come before story. Developers often view story incorrectly: as an after-thought that can bend awkwardly to the whims of tech, art., etc. It is the case, therefore, that storytelling can result in a stagnant form, with little to no opportunities for branching narrative, little to no variations in character points of view upon a second replay. Story, in execution, can be expensive, for it requires numerous and appropriate mechanisms to deliver it. If you look to video games, for example, execution of story can require: live actors for motion capture animation or professional voice over to create mini cinematics (aka cut scenes); digital collectibles that break from the gameplay; on-screen text to justify or explain missions; and more. Other interactive media, which can embrace many of video games' story mechanisms, confront similar cost-prohibitive endeavors that will make the *story experience* better, but not critical or even necessary to the overall *interactive experience*.

For the platforms addressed in this book, story comprises the traditional components that, well, make a story a story, for example: character, structure, tone, theme, etc. Storytelling's current form redefines the location/social nature status for most of these platforms. Without it, most of these platforms would fail to have a clear designation within the location/social nature model.

A FINAL NOTE

By way of their experience and insight, the contributors of this book aim to explain their respective creative landscape and equip the reader with the best approaches to tackling a creative challenge in said landscape. I've contributed my own article, focusing on a complementary perspective (entitled "Red Flags"). While it's critical to learn about best practices, so too is it important to develop the filter and intuition for warning signs and questionable business decisions that typically saddle a company undertaking a game-changing experience or innovation. The intersection of entertainment and technology – the primary setting of this book – welcomes as many exciting opportunities as it does challenges. Thus, to be a great storyteller in this world is to be a vigilant one.

Ross Berger

CHAPTER 1

Virtual Assistants and Storytelling

Flint Dille and Zane Dille

CONTENTS

INTRODUCTION

Ross Berger asked me an interesting question: can virtual assistants ("VAs") such as Alexa and Siri become stand-out storytelling platforms in and of themselves? More specifically, what new mode of storytelling can emerge from VAs that stands outside of recycling previous entertainment products with minor adaptations to the platform?

I picture a thought balloon opening up over my head, and there's nothing in it. Empty. That's always an interesting way to start a journey, without a fixed idea or preconceptions. Traditionally, writers don't like looking at the blank page – there's a reason that the most common piece of advice handed out to aspiring writers is to just write something, start somewhere, and work from there. I didn't get that brain, no more than I got the polishing or editing brain. What follows is a type of document I've never quite written before. More thought experiment and pitch than academic research.

DOI: 10.1201/9781003141594-2

Let's start out with a blanket statement. Despite spending no small part of my career writing children's entertainment, I'm not interested in talking about children's entertainment on Alexa, Siri, or Cortana, because I want to avoid anything that enables lazy parents. Instead, I want to flip the replacement paradigm, the tendency for technology to supplant human connections. What do the bedtime stories we heard as children grow up to be, and what are we for having been imbued with them?

I never understood where my ability to write goofy cartoon humor came from. Total mystery to me. I was the only person in the animation business who didn't know the difference between the Warner Brothers characters and the Disney characters when I was hired to write a movie that grew up to be the *Tiny Toons* TV series. I'd watched the normal cartoons everybody else watched when I was a kid, and nothing more. I didn't even think I particularly liked them.

Yet, oddly, I was able to write cartoon sequences and, even more oddly, people liked them. It was a whole off-ramp of my career, through multiple movies unmade and ones that did get made, like *Fievel Goes West*.

And yet it was effortless, and I eventually figured out why. It was my grandmother. Both of my parents and my sister were good bedtime storytellers, but my grandmother was something I never quite encountered again. She'd start a story about Mrs. O'Leary's cow. It would kick over a lantern and *almost* start the Chicago fire (I'm from Chicago), but the flame would give a cat a hot paw and the cat would shriek, causing the mice to scatter and, in turn, causing the elephants in the Lincoln Park Zoo to stampede, who would then be so thirsty that they drank out of Buckingham Fountain and used their trunks as hoses to put out the fire. But then the water would flood, causing a river that the beavers would have to dam really fast with the help of woodpeckers cutting down trees.

You get the idea. She had a free association Rube Goldberg of a story that could go on and on forever. I'd laugh and laugh and laugh. When I had an idea, she'd add it in and off we'd go.

The driving force behind these ridiculous stories, and the ones I later gave a try at telling, was enchantment. She would take a basic fact, that beavers dam rivers, and imbue it with magic and creativity until it was part of an outrageous tale. The same force drove a lot of the projects I worked on later: imbuing cars with personalities until they became *The Transformers*, making museums and sculptures part of an interplanetary struggle in *Ingress*, and, perhaps most strangely, creating a competitive platform for collaboration with DARPA that we called *Polyplexus*.

My goal, then, is to figure out how we can use VAs as everyday enchanters that turn quotidian experiences into memorable parts of our narrative lives, enhancing and transforming us.

THE PLATFORM

Let's look at VAs like we would look at any other emerging medium. What are the strong suits of VAs for storytelling, what are the weak suits, and how do you leverage the strong to outshine other mediums?

VAs have been with us for a while now. They started slow, in the 1960s, as verbal interfaces that replicated what we could or would do with a keyboard on a calculator (IBM Shoebox) or computer (chatbot ELIZA). In the 1990s, VAs made possible speech-recognition software such as Dragon Naturally Speaking and interactive voice response systems that provided automated telephone replies for callers who sought help with their bank or hospital. Then, in 2011, a certain VA became a household name thanks to smart phones. Remember when Siri first picked up interest, answering trivial questions with often comical results? Humor and entertainment were key parts of the transition to VAs being normal, accessible, understandable. Then, VAs wandered into the car, filling a niche where we couldn't – or more, shouldn't – do things the old way. Then, we started linking it to our houses, to the bits we thought were analog and unchanging. Turning on the lights, starting the music (and picking it for us, when we were indecisive), finding the movie we were looking for and where to stream it. These were the visible changes, the noticeable, "huh, this is easier" moments.

The next paradigm shift was when VAs started helping us make decisions as much as helping us enact them. They started to know what music we like, what topics we're interested in, what mundane responses we give to emails we didn't really want to read. "Excellent, thank you." "Thursday works." Seeing those sorts of things happen reminds me of when I'd see my kids doing things that I didn't know they could do. Take a second and think about the implications of a technology that can read your emails and understand them well enough to give you multiple responses to them and know you well enough to know which is the most likely.

For narrative, VAs have been used to narrate pick-a-path stories. This is not very surprising – nearly every medium starts with pick-a-path stories. Paperback pick-a-paths were huge in the 1980s with titles like "Endless Quest" and "Choose Your Own Adventure" and so on. They were aimed at children, because children are early adopters by nature and pick-a-paths are good for bedtime reading, due to the fact that they have choices that the reader and the listener can enjoy together. Since then, we've had pick-paths on CD-ROMS, on text-based computer games, on the more modern Telltale Games experiences, and so forth.

But let's step forward from there by looking at the mechanics involved and seeing what else we can do with them. Siri can be a storyteller, but Siri can also be a companion as we go through the story, playing an advisor like Dean Stockdale in *Quantum Leap*, blurring the lines between coach, friend, and fellow traveler.

VAs sit at the nexus between the vast stores of ever-updating information on the internet and real-time data on their users' lives. On the one hand, VAs know everything from the weather to coffee shops nearby to where there will be live music tonight and what the coolest new museum exhibit is. In other words, VAs are capable of populating a game world with thousands of interactions and places to go and sights to see. Simultaneously, Siri knows what the weather conditions are on days I walk more than 10,000 steps and which coffee shops I already like and what music I've been listening to lately and everywhere I already have been and everything I already have seen. This is the unique niche VAs can fill: the same way my grandmother could use her knowledge that beavers build dams to set up a comical water-overrun resolution, a VA can use its attenuation to those two streams of data as narrative resources to draw upon. The next question is then: what does the process between knowing stuff and imbuing it with narrative magic look like?

For that, I'm going to take a step back to what drives us in narrative and games.

PROPULSION LOOPS

One more principle before we dive in to using VAs for narrative.

There is no clear line between storytelling and game designing. A story is a game played between teller and listener. The teller has options, either in how they write or how they read, to try and intrigue the reader; the reader can let his interest show, can decide at any point whether it's worth it to keep listening or keep reading, and so forth. The social benefit of VA storytelling, however, rests on shifting from the compulsion loop of all gaming (whether it's logging in for a daily quest or grinding for a new ability) to a propulsion loop.

One of the things we discovered early on at Google,[1] working on *Ingress*, was that, after playing a real-world game where they walked around capturing portal after portal, players were suddenly realizing that their lives had changed. They were going outside, getting exercise, meeting new people, having new adventures, and literally seeing the world around them in a whole new way. One early player summed it up on a Google+ (remember that?) post, saying he'd lost 20 pounds, had a whole new set of friends, and, because of the Alternate Reality story, was suddenly caring about history and events more than he ever had. This was fascinating. The "Compulsion Loop," which usually sounds like drug addiction, had turned into a "Propulsion Loop" powering him into a better life.

More recently, working on a DARPA project called *Polyplexus*, which is envisioned as a gamified social network for scientists and engineers to speed up innovation, we are attempting to turn the "compulsion" loop that drives games, social media, and clickbait into something that benefits the object of them – and, in the case of DARPA, science. Our theory is that, like the *Ingress* player, we could reward players with levelling and badges to do things that would give them more knowledge, connections, and insights. In the broadest possible sense, we are treating scientific quests like games and stories and challenging them to "beat" them through Invention and Innovation while backing it with rigorous science. The jury is still out on whether this will work, but it looks promising.

So, to the extent that our gamified storytelling motivates and informs users to improve their lives, we are doing a social good, on the theory that if individuals propel themselves, then it is a good for society.

WHAT'S COMING NEXT?

I do not have a lot to say about the production cycle of a VA storytelling experience. My suggestion is that the cycle starts with the low-hanging fruit: "Pick-a-path Adventure with Alexa," or some such, and gradually build out and gamify from there. Start the game part with a Mandelbrot set of rules and expand from there. As every game designer has discovered, emergent behavior will fill the holes.

It's important for a new player to be up and running and having fun within 5 minutes (or you're dead) and yet there needs to be enough

---

[1] This was before Niantic, Inc. – the studio that created *Ingress* – was spun off as its own entity in 2015. Prior to that, it was an internal startup at Google known as Niantic Labs. – R.B.

complexity to keep players interested and coming back. Part of that will come from adding more "content," adding more of what the player *already* likes, and part of that will come from adding features, functions, and options, adding more for the player *to* like.

The live-or-die of any game is play-testing. Games, by their very nature, are complex, semi-predictable endeavors. Stories are the same thing. Writers take a simple set of rules and keep retooling them in new and exciting ways. But there must be rules or the audience will have no idea what they're watching. If it's too rule-based, too predictable, the users will get bored.

The plot, characters, style, and theme of any story might come from the brain of the creator: how about "let's make an anti-capitalist game where the goal is to make a monopoly and bankrupt the other players." Sounds fun enough. But what nobody saw coming was the varied styles of Free Parking or "$400 when you land on Go." As themed editions of the game entered the marketplace over time, players went from anti-capitalism to "voting money out of the public treasuries." Does it wreck the intended balance of *Monopoly*? Maybe. Do people seem to find it more fun? Absolutely.

And this is true of stories. We might think we're writing about one thing, but those pesky readers have a habit of seeing something else. Upton Sinclair thought he was writing a tirade about child labor when he had a kid fall into a meat processing machine, but he ended up causing the founding of the FDA. "I wanted to touch their hearts, but I kicked them in their stomachs." Should he have known that the taboo against cannibalism would override compassion? Maybe.

Suppose you want to move beyond pick-a-path adventures. The next step will be VAs as experience coordinators. Consider the layer between pick-a-path adventures and the real-world facsimiles (dinner theatre and murder mystery parties and so forth). Imagine a murder mystery party with lights going on and off in different rooms, conversations starting and ending of their own accord in each room (in each scene). Sounds come from different places. We hear the pouring rain and the rushing wind; we can hear ghosts in the attic. Merge VAs with augmented reality and now people and things can manifest anywhere. A body really can appear in the room you're calling the conservatory for the night. An alien base really can appear on the beach. The game developers supply the world and the story, but the players provide the characters – except, of course, the VAs are the NPCs (nonplayable characters).

Story design starts out with some assumptions about your potential audience. These can be simple. "Our potential players like fantasy," or "Our potential players are into mysteries." We can start out with some basic assumptions:

1. They are going to be early adopters, by definition. Early adopters are rare creatures. The trick here, in a social game set in the real world, will be creating a game not only for the early adopters but for the people they drag along to the experience. The temptation is always to do things for children because they are happy early adopters. We don't have to start there. In the modern world, where every esoteric interest has thousands or millions of followers, we can mine early adopters from other places too.

2. The question to answer is "what's the fun?" for different player types. For instance, if you're doing a murder mystery dinner party, a certain amount of the people involved will be people who just like going to dinner parties. The mystery adds a hook and an ambience but won't be perceived as fun if it breaks the social experience.

3. *World of Warcraft* uses the Bartle Test to assess different kinds of players – the big four are explorers, achievers, killers, and socializers, and each player can be ranked in each category. The genius of *WoW* is that the further you go, the more you evolve. You find yourself socializing more in the interludes between raid pulls, you find yourself exploring because you meant to be grinding for herbs, and so forth. So, a VA dinner party would have solvers, socializers, actors, and organizers.

There are a lot more assumptions to make, and for a lot more cases – the murder mystery dinner is just a useful heuristic – but let's then look to the challenges:

a. How do you get a complete noob up and running inside 5 minutes? What is the immediate fun thing to do? How will every player know what to do right away? Do we include prompts? (Ask Professor Plum about his relationship with Mrs. White). What is the simple path that keeps people going? Have a simple goal for every player. Find the killer? Stop the killer before they kill you? You are the killer?

Commit the murder and throw shade on everybody else. Whatever. Everybody needs to know what they're doing.

The point is to leverage VAs to help every player through the game and, maybe, to slow down the people who are getting it too fast. The goal is not to manage a competition as much as to make sure everybody is having a good time. If users are falling behind, they get hints. One of the fascinating things about psychology I've observed is that people don't remember getting hints and often think they figured things out for themselves. Take advantage of the fact that you are leveraging a familiar genre. Decide whether you're going to "brand" it with a mystery writer or a pre-existing intellectual property. It could be the Agatha Christie game or *Knives Out Again*. Or dodge the I.P. issue and make your own. There are good arguments for both strategies, but that's outside the scope of this chapter.

b. How does tech figure in? Suppose you're doing a "Dark and Stormy Night" premise. Does the game come with VA active "lightning flashers?" And what about the thunder? Is everybody wearing earbuds or do you assume a single phone hooked up to speakers? In the case of this project, no small part of the game will be the sale and promotion of VA peripherals.

In other words, if the story begins with the victim reading his will on a video from beyond the grave, is the game dependent on a TV that can run the video? Where does the video live? Is it on the internet? Is it on the phone? The real question is how much tech you assume the player has, and if the player doesn't have the tech, does that preclude them from playing?

And, as with any real-world product, you have to make assumptions about the player's environment. Do they have enough different rooms to go into? Can it be played in a one-room apartment?

c. Is there some market or use that we're not thinking about? Is this a game for resorts or hotels to amuse their guests and sell food and wine on the way? All decisions have to be discussed upon the outset.

d. Payoff: Don't rule out the possibility that character activities can be recorded and the night's adventure can be turned into its own linear book, complete with pictures, if picture taking is included in the story. What a fascinating artifact of a fun night.

And this triggers another possibility. Since our VA can control cameras, can the story be automatically videoed and edited to produce the equivalent of a show or movie about your game? Something to think about.

Now, back to reality: "What will happen?" Any time there is a new medium, people will do all of the following things. (And if it sounds like I'm mocking them, well, that's accurate but as I do so, I have to fully disclose that I've been on almost every snipe hunt that the "tech meets entertainment" business has gone on in the last three or so decades.)

- A conga-line of developers will start doing "edutainment" products. Most will fail miserably, but they will be considered noble failures.

- A few art-damaged, esoteric things will come out. They'll be highly praised and lowly sold.

- There will be well-intentioned failures.

- There will be a jewel or maybe a couple.

- Everybody will have learned a lot.

VIRTUAL VIRGIL

The "Dark and Stormy Night" style of idea uses a lot more of the platform's potential than the crop of Pick-a-Paths and Edutainment products, but it still isn't tapping into every capability VAs have. As VAs become more built-out platforms and designers start to get creative, VAs will operate as experience coordinators for augmented reality games played out in the real world. There's one last phase that strikes me off the bat: what happens when the gameplay doesn't need the augmented reality overlay?

Think of VAs as a dungeon master for your life and quotidian existence. A virtual Virgil who leads you through the Inferno, Purgatorio, and Paradiso of the real world every day, or any time you want him to. And this Virgil knows who you are, where you are, what you want, when things are happening around you, which of your friends are around, and why you are playing. Imagine harnessing the power of all of that.

To describe how this works, in real life and in the real world, I have a trainer named Dennis. Dennis was a college football star and played in the pros until injury cut short his career. Now he is a personal trainer. He's got a unique business. His entire gym is in his van (on some days, his pick-up) and he trains in public parks. He models his training on football training. That's the layer of fantasy. As I'm long past the age of ever dreaming of being in the NFL or playing any kind of football other than maybe touch or *Madden*, we all know this is a layer of fantasy, but it works. We talk about football during the season. In other words, while I'm lifting real weights and doing dig routes, I am fantasizing about a football career that will never happen. Fantasy is promoting a new reality. During COVID, I added a couple inches to my shoulders. Fantasy input. Real world results.

I'm quite sure that I'm not the only person in the world who does this. Coachified bike riding has made Peloton one of the star companies of the COVID-era and I'm sure that people in Zumba classes fantasize about being professional dancers. Very few of them will be appearing in the Bolshoi Ballet, but that's not the point. They're levelling themselves up.

Take that to the next level. Suppose we blur the actual player's identity with a fantasy goal they might have. In the same way that Google news data-mines me to figure out what I am interested in and, more specifically, which client's products to sell me, suppose your VA proactively knows what you want – or better yet – your VA can game you into a better life. You're interested in wine and want to know more about it, it will tell you when there's a tasting nearby or when you're driving past a winery or when there's a class or lecture that might be of interest to you either online or nearby.

Ah... And somebody on your contact list who's also interested in wine is only a block away, but neither of you would know it... But Virgil, our semi omniscient VA, does know it and arranges a meet-up. Puppet-mastered arranged serendipity.

Your VA will also level you and give you badges and awards, but the real reward is that you actually do become knowledgeable about wine over time.

This is propulsive gamification for real life. It is allowing us to become a semifictional character to optimize ourselves. And here's the payoff. The better you get at it, the more you become like your aspirational fictional character.

There's another angle to approach from too. And that's the enchantment of the mundane. Have you ever been sitting at a bar making conversation and you start speculating outrageously about the lives of the people around you?

CLOSING

Some mad scientist's concoction of witches' brews of these concepts will be the winner. The experimentation is going to be the journey. And do not assume the answer is going to be just one thing any more than the final uses of film and video are just one thing. We have movies, television shows, now streaming television shows, commercials, documentaries, animated films – and so on. The point here is don't assume that there's going to be just one answer.

Do assume that there are going to be a lot of edutainment snipe hunts.

Probably the best model for what the snipe hunts will look like is the CD-ROM/MULTIMEDIA era. For those of you who are too young to remember it and those of you who have worked hard to forget it, this was one huge epic fail of an era to try and figure out how to monetize this "breakthrough new technology."

Rarely have I seen such a spectacular crash as Christmas of, I think, 1996 when my local Borders Bookstore (remember those?) stocked up with CD-ROM products (one of them, mine) and expected to change the world. They ranged from what was called "shovelware" (let's put our encyclopedia on CD-ROM and people will be really happy to wait endlessly and run into painfully short articles), to weird artsy projects disguised as education where nobody could really figure out how to use them, to small animated projects that didn't go anywhere – and so on.

By February, they were all in the remainder bin. *Myst* seemed to be the only successful game, and that was simultaneously an incredibly ingenious and incredibly dull "find the backstory" game.

No offense to anybody here. I'll throw *Zork* into this mix too.

Meanwhile, CD-ROMS took off on the (then) new PlayStation and found a home there. Their descendants (games on DVDs) are very much still around.

And while that era can seem like a laughable search for smokebenders, shoreline, and skyhooks, the truth is that it netted the basic language protocols of the internet. The language we use every day on the internet. Just look at those silly projects and the internet now, and all of the protocols for interacting between a mouse and screen were figured out back then.

So as much as we want to laugh at that period and the Silicon Valley/ Hollywood (aka Sillywood) collaborations of the day, the world we now live in is built on the wreckage of those silly experiments. The lesson here is don't necessarily look at the content or the actual products but look at where they're going. Follow the right birdy.

Most of the VA entertainment products will be bad. Expect a journey of thinly disguised "shovelware" and lots of "brand slapping" (people will love it if, for example, it's Marvel even if the product fell out the back of a horse). There will be flawed "educational" products; there will be weird art-damaged oddities. I just thought of my own: a "sound bed" for your life. A mood matcher that adds a soundtrack from your home speakers, giving your house fountain and rain sound effects while pastoral poetry plays from your buds or your speakers when your Apple Watch thinks your heart rate is too high.

But it's okay. If there's one thing that breaks out, it's worth it. We've changed the world. I could make a good argument that *Myst* was a breakthrough in what we now call "Worldbuilding" (another term I'm getting sick of, but not quite as sick as I am of "Storytelling").

If there's not, the lessons learned here will help some future medium. Breakthrough successes are built on the backs of lots of experiments, some successful, some failed. And these journeys are always worth taking because they always force new thought. My best tip? Siri or Alexa can turn your life into an exciting story in which you are the main character... Figure out what that means and you're a billionaire.

CHAPTER 2

Writing for Toys – Actually a Job

Rob Auten

CONTENTS

THE TITLE OF THE essay is a response to the question most frequently asked when I mention having written for toys. For many people, apparently, the idea that toys require content or an author is confusing. This is understandable as the conventional definition of toys, as any Montessori graduate will tell you, is enablers rather than arbiters of play. Some play purists consider the very idea of content creation for a toy to be anathema. Should you presently be engaged as a writer on a toy, this may explain some of the looks you've been getting in the cafeteria, but it doesn't get around the fact that toys, and particularly technology-powered toys, are growing rapidly and that someone must create content for them. If you should be so fortunate as to find yourself with a toy in need of content or in a content-creation role for a toy, this chapter is for you.

DOI: 10.1201/9781003141594-3

Should you simply be curious about the manner in which toys can tell stories, or remain suspicious about the thesis implied by this article's title, I shall begin by illustrating the ways in which toys act as narrative objects. Should you be convinced or find this material relevant to your practice, the remainder of this discussion focuses on some of the methodology surrounding the creative process, offering insights that hopefully are of use.

HOW TOYS TELL STORIES

The historically primary manner through which toys have told stories is as artifacts from a larger world. The first "action figures" were Hasbro's *G.I. Joe* figures, based on a sobriquet prevalent in American culture since the end of the Second World War. A media theorist might consider these toys[1] the first transmedia objects, leaving the cynic to bemoan the contemporary imagination's inability to play without a related linear narrative to serve as an example. Certainly, there is a connection between toys and the emerging discipline known as "worldbuilding," which unites physical objects with digital or linear media in the attempt to create a polyvalent world that can be entered through a variety of means (and at a variety of price points). In this arrangement, the media performs the lion's share of the storytelling while the toy exists as the vehicle for creative, albeit informed, play.

While there are myriad examples of comics, animation, film, and even products (e.g., Kellogg's *Tony the Tiger* plushies) becoming toys, there is a business-driven shift toward interactions between the digital and physical that allow the digital components to shape the narrative around the play action. This began in "toys to life" video games, an early example of which (though not known by this term) was Nintendo's R.O.B. robot. This confusing appellation describes a system in which when the toy does something, the world (in this case, the one within the video game) reacts. Familiar examples of this include the *Skylanders* series – also a series of books, comics, and a Netflix animated series – and Nintendo's "Amiibo" figurines. It won't be long before toys are far more adept at collaboration and personalized responses, hopefully in a manner that sparks (rather than smothers) the creative impulse.

---

[1] More specifically, the *G.I. Joe: A Real American Hero* toyline and its corresponding animation show and comic book series. The 1982 premiere of these action figures, 3¾ inches in length, marked a major departure from its 12-inch precursor that first hit the market in 1963. –R.B.

Despite the increased focus on interdependence across media formats, toys are typically delivered with a narrative context that can be essential to their popularity. Action figures often include a mini-dossier on the package's inhabitants, as well as framing text that underlines the core conflict and factions within the toy's world. This material provides context for play, both by helping define the capabilities of the toy within its fantasy world and by explaining the "why" that makes the toy feel important. In the world of the *Transformers*, for example, knowing that the Autobots and Decepticons are locked in a vicious struggle that will determine Earth's fate lends a touch of gravitas to a car that is also a robot. This information is likely to alter the way the toy is used (more mashing/laser noises, less racing) and will provide a frame for the stories that emerge.

There are, additionally, toys that are created as storytelling systems. You may recall toys such as Teddy Ruxpin (essentially a cassette player capable of triggering the servo-powered movements of a teddy bear), Hello Barbie (a chatbot housed within a fashion doll), or Sphero's Interactive Spiderman (a chatbot housed within a "big head" figurine). Disney created Playmation, a toy system based around an expandable collection of smart action figures and *Avengers*-themed wearable storytelling devices that were capable of tracking actions, from walking to hiding to making noise. Not all storytelling toys need to be as extensive or complex. There is a defensible case to be made for a Tamagotchi as a narrative device, or even the 1970s Talking View-Master. While these toys may be part of larger worlds, their primary function is to give the player agency within a narrative and to shape that world around the actions and decisions made by that player.

PLAY IS PERSONAL

Below, I'll offer some advice on creating content for toys. Some of what I say may be relevant to creating content in other media, but it is important to remember that things that work in media in general, and even in other forms of interactive media such as video or board games, are not necessarily applicable to toys. Toys and play are like the young Marlon Brando when it comes to tearing down existing structures of rules and logic. Even when a toy has a clear function within a known story world, a player will often ignore these rules and employ the toy in a manner that never could have been anticipated by its creators. In the comics that bear his name, Wolverine does not attend many tea parties. He has never tended to Baby Yoda or been the butler to a Disney Princess, but he has doubtlessly served these roles and many more in households and imaginations around the world. Dolls, figurines, and stuffed animals have been a part of our play vocabulary for thousands of years and will likely stay in vogue for quite a while because they so easily accept the whims of their mercurial masters. As a creator, you must imagine your intended personas for the product you are creating, but you will do yourself a service by additionally attempting to understand how your toy will be misused and ensuring that you aren't getting between your audience and their intentions. This makes toys somewhat unique in the pantheon of play, as other forms of play (such as video games) have established the use of guardrails to ensure adherence to their internal logic.

QUICK QUALIFICATIONS

Before we enter a more granular discussion about the creative process, bear with me a moment as I provide some personal context. I have spent most of the last 20 years creating content, overseeing its delivery, and supervising other content creators for a variety of interactive mediums, including video games, theme park attractions, escape rooms, virtual reality doodads, cruise ships, animations, and toys. The greatest lesson I have pulled from working in these varying formats is that writing for each is just like every other form of interactive writing until it isn't. This is perhaps best exemplified by toy creation, as the most innovative and interesting toys are often captivating because they are clearly delineated from what already exists in the market.

This means that while I could write you a quick few thousand words on "How to write a compelling first-person shooter" in a manner dry and formulaic enough to come out of Escoffier, the signposts in my possession for toy creation are far less precisely hewn. Instead, I'll offer a set of guidelines within which you'll have to find the solutions that fit your particular problem. Apologies if this is disappointing, but we are playing within a very broad playing field. If you're looking for something more definitive, there are of course other resources (within this very book), but I would counsel that it is unlikely that the specific solutions of others will fix the problems that you're currently facing. For the moment, tell yourself that it's possible you'll come out of this essay less fraught with anxiety than you were going into it, and let's get to work.

KNOWING THE AUDIENCE

If you are also the creator or designer of the toy in question, you have likely already considered the intended user or users of your creation. In larger workplaces, this message doesn't always make its way to the content creators, often because people have the tendency to think the user is obvious. So, if you have not already been provided with documentation about your intended users, you should immediately seek some out. If it doesn't exist, politely ask why. Inexperienced designers sometimes cling to the idea that a toy is for "everyone" and that, therefore, consideration of the user is unnecessary. While it is not your job to disabuse anyone of their silly and naive assumptions, you will want to, even if you must do so quietly, create a few user personas that you can consider as you are creating content. Typically, these will involve "casting" a few imaginary people as potential users. Let your imagination run wild when creating these imaginary users and try to give special consideration to people who may not share your background or experiences. As mentioned above, consider the users who will be using the toy outside of its intended design and attempt also not to consider them "wrong."

Though you are encouraged to make elements of these user stories as expansive as you like, you will also want to have a "baseball card" for each that you can conveniently keep on hand throughout the content creation process. As you are working on your scenarios, occasionally choose a card at random and ask yourself how this user would experience the content you are creating. It is more than fine if you think they might not find it all that appealing. (It is not your job to make everyone equally happy all of the time.) But if you find you have a persona who is almost never happy, or are creating content that doesn't seem like it would much appeal to anyone, you will want to consider some changes.

SECOND FIDDLER

If you are creating content for a toy, it is probable that at least some of what you are attempting to convey constitutes a story. This may be a story that you have made up in the shower or it may be a tale beloved by millions over generations. Your job is to get it over with quickly. No matter how this story is being told, be it in an instruction book or an audio prompt, it is a distraction from the toy's prime directive, which is to be fun to play with. You, with your important story to tell, are the literal killjoy who is ruining that play experience. If your address was written on the back of the box, you would get letters addressed to "Stick in the Mud." Therefore, provided you do not find repugnance in the joy of others, you want to get whatever it is you have to say out of the way as quickly as possible. This is true on both a macro and micro level, as the examples below shall attempt to illustrate.

Let's start by looking at the function of your narrative. When creating for any interactive environment, language primarily exists to either inform the audience of a piece of information they will hopefully find interesting or instruct the audience on a method to achieve a defined goal. Anything not in these two categories should be put under the microscope and considered deeply. Having a character tell a shaggy dog story because you find it charming or funny is deeply disrespectful to your audience. Kids won't get it and adults, many of whom may only have limited time and patience to participate in play activities, will resent you. Worse, you will teach your users that your product is confusing and pretentious. Being brief, letting imagination fill gaps, and facilitating dialogue between player and plaything allow for a better balance between your message and the player's interests.

PROVIDING VALUE

Once you've smoothed out the storytelling, consider the manner in which information is being communicated. Whereas books, films, television, and even fortune cookies can operate under the assumption that the audience is paying attention to what they have to say, this attentive largesse does not apply to the toy-employing masses. This means that you need to prioritize which messages are most important and the tools in your possession are best suited to communicate them.

For example, let's say you're creating content for a (hypothetical) storytelling robot. For whatever reason, the design of this darling automaton is such that it can't talk when it's lying on its stomach. Therefore, should the device be placed on its stomach and unable to function, the method through which it expresses itself should feel more immediate than when it is regaling you with stories from its days in robot college. How this works in practice is something that you and the designers will have to work out, but a holistic understanding of context should lead to a rational sense of priority.

Generally speaking, you are likely to have a few types of content. Some content must be understood in order for the player to feel successful, such as the downward-dogging robot above. Not every toy will have this, but should you be working on a project that does contain imperative information, make sure you have a way of either presenting it with some additional emphasis or repeating it clearly in a manner that clarifies the causality between the cessation of frustration and the information presently being presented.

INSTRUCTING EFFICIENTLY

The art of giving directions is one of the most important skills in the content creator's toolkit, and the previous discussion (re: brevity) is doubly essential herein. However tempted you may be toward wordplay or clever language, the primary function of an instruction is that it should be easy to understand. This means clarity above all things. Think of directions as a structured form of poetry, in which the goal is to get each word to make as much impact as possible. For example:

Muddy: "Uh-oh… Looks like we're at one minute to midnight. I guess this would probably be a good time to go ahead and press the red button or whatever."
Clear: "Emergency! To avoid death, press the red button!"

Obviously, you may not be able to be quite as concise with every toy and every character, but hopefully the point has been made. There are a few things to additionally consider when writing instructions, such as the order of the motive and the request. Even though it may seem a little unnatural at times, it is generally a good rule to first identify the situation that the player may wish to change before, then tell them the methodology that must be employed in order to change it. What happens here is that the brain recognizes that the information being presented is relevant, which causes it to perk up and catch the actual instruction.

For example, part of the reason for the tense relationship between Catherine Martin and Buffalo Bill, as depicted in the film *Silence of the Lambs*, may have been because Buffalo Bill wasn't particularly effective at phrasing his instructions. When he tells Catherine, "It puts the lotion on its skin or else it gets the hose again," she may be distracted or otherwise disinclined to pay attention until Bill mentions the stimulus she would prefer to avoid. A more effective way to phrase the request, while still maintaining the linguistic idiosyncrasies of the character, would be to say, "To avoid getting the hose again, it puts the lotion on its skin."

EVERY PLAYER MATTERS

The act of playing is an act of individual expression. While playing, I am having a unique, majestic experience. I am the ruler sitting upon the throne of my kingdom and the director of my own movie. The stories that you tell should be in service to this fantasy, and as a storyteller you must make peace with the fact that you are not working in a medium in which writerly virtues are praised above all others. Your job is to construct the ramp from which the Evel Knievel of the imagination launches. If you do your job well, all eyes will be on the motorcycle flying through the air, save for those of your fellow ramp-smiths, who will nod to you respectfully.

In service of fun, consider the variety of ways in which you can inspire activity. Toys are at their best when players are pulling and pushing and plonking and plinking. They are items which activities can be done with rather than done to. If the toy is dictating how it is to be used, it will be interesting only for as long as it is novel. And once the toy loses its novelty, it is typically either discarded or, in the case of the more enterprising players, disassembled. You may, for example, want to compare your toy to an object often employed as a toy, such as couch cushions or a large cardboard box. These objects offer little narrative provocation and can be utilized in play scenarios from jungle cave to space station to Grand Prix racer. If your content is consistently restricting the potential for plurality of function, you are in danger of finding your toy cast aside.

EXTENDING THE EXPERIENCE

Many video games start by giving the player a taste of what it is like to be a massively powered entity and then strip those powers away, allowing the player to unlock them gradually over the course of hours of gameplay. If your toy has the ability to hint at content or capabilities that lie ahead, don't be afraid to play that very powerful card. Having a clear sense of play progression is important (though ensure that any "plan" that you have for the player is invisible), and interjecting elements of surprise into that plan will help maintain player interest.

This sense of progression should also be applied to any difficulty settings your toy may possess. Ideally, you want to be training players in the development of a new skill and then giving them the opportunity to feel as if they are mastering that skill. Switching between skills helps ensure that no one skill is forgotten, but ensure you tweak the difficulty to be slightly easier than it was just prior to switching away from the skill in order to help the player ease back into things. In general, the level of difficulty should aim to consistently be challenging enough to be captivating without becoming frustrating. It's like a great conversation with a new friend, in which you're learning about one another's skills and interests.

LEAVING ROOM

Toys are like people in that we often have complex relationships with them. This is because we put some of ourselves in them (and love in the toy with what we narcissistically love in ourselves), but the clever creator will be able to imbue their creation with some of its own personality. This, however, should rarely be *your* personality. As wonderful as you certainly are, the role of creator has given you the opportunity to create a character or a voice that's even more charming and interesting or beguiling. Consider the relationship between the toy and its owner and realize that this is something that you can shape from afar. While different toys are designed to serve different functions, you pretty much can't go wrong by creating something that is beloved. If your user is a child, you want to create the toy that doesn't get thrown out after its owner "grows up." This may be because it is so cute, so funny, so evocative, so scary, or so silly. As long as it is doing what it does better than other products attempting to pluck the same chord, the toy will continue to hold a place in the hearts of its audience.

Part of what makes writing for toys so interesting is the potential to create something deeply meaningful for your audience. There is a responsibility inherent in this, as you are now responsible, in part, for the development of your player's imagination. By respecting each member of your audience and supporting them in their adventures, you are transforming a product into a companion. You are holding them by the hand as they embark upon a journey in which you have created together. When done well, there are few forms of creation as entrancing or inspiring.

CHAPTER 3

Approaching Virtual Reality Storytelling

Sarah Beaulieu

CONTENTS

*N*OTE: *FOR THE PURPOSES of this article, I will focus mainly on works of fiction. Also, virtual reality ("VR") does not refer to 360° videos, even though some paragraphs can apply to the latter.*

For a few years now, VR has entered our homes. With the progressive democratization of this relatively new medium, jobs are emerging, among them: writers and narrative designers. They are entering the world of VR while still in the process of defining their narrative tools. Because it sits at the crossroads of screenwriting, playwriting, interactive writing, narrative design, and even filmmaking, VR storytelling is a wide land to roam for storytellers.

DOI: 10.1201/9781003141594-4

Like any medium at its early stage, virtual reality borrows from other media to begin identifying its own specificities and progressively define its unique language, also known as *remediation*.[1] Based on this logic, writers coming from cinema, video games, or theater try to tame VR storytelling by applying what they already know about the art of crafting stories in their respective medium to VR, with the final aim of transforming this knowledge into an independent new form of storytelling.

But because a VR experience cannot be reduced to the experience of a story, writing for VR cannot be reduced to *writing a story*. Sometimes, a VR experience focuses on the user sensations brought by environments or sounds themselves, more than the series of events which traditionally make up a story. Therefore, writing for VR does not always mean writing characters, plot points, and dialogue; it means designing an experience as a whole, considering player agency, connecting mechanics with narrative, and taking into account all the specificities of VR, among other things. When approaching this new field, writers (especially ones coming from noninteractive media) must then understand what it means to set up a narrative for an interactive medium driven by specific constraints.

Since the mid-1980s, the word *immersive* is used to define one of the specificities of virtual reality. Here, *immersion* refers to the sensation experienced by the users of *diving* into a 3D virtual world, a sensation that mainly comes from the fact that there is no interface between the user and the images generated by the device. By reproducing a perception of reality, VR can generate a strong sensorial experience.

Immersion may be one of the reasons why VR is so attractive to storytellers: being able to completely *immerse* a user into our story world is a dream come true. But to create and maintain a coherent 3D virtual world, graphics, sounds, point of view, and interactions must work together. Therefore, understanding the mechanics of immersion[2] to write for VR is like understanding the game mechanics and the player's agency to write for video games: it is essential to deliver a good narrative.

Some stories are better told on screen. Others are better suited for literature, radio, or video games. If VR is the right medium for your project, you will know by answering a few simple questions: *Why* <u>must</u> *I tell my story*

---

[1] Manovitch, Lev. *The Language of New Media.* (Cambridge: MIT Press, 2001).

[2] In VR, the user feels physically present in the virtual world. This is immersion.

in this medium? What will VR bring to the narrative? How can I exploit the specificities of VR to carry out my story, world, characters, theme, point of view? If you are struggling to answer these, the following paragraphs should help you, starting from the beginning: identifying the creative and technical constraints of your project.

IDENTIFY THE NARRATIVE MEANS

VR offers a wide range of experiences. When starting a VR project, whatever it might be, you will soon face constraints at all levels and will have to make decisions depending on various factors: the type of experience you are creating, budget limitations, technical constraints, creative direction, art direction, team structure, and sometimes even marketing or studio guidelines.

When you define your narrative means – or narrative tools – at an early stage, you have to keep those constraints and directions in mind. This is major since you will build your plot, characters, and story world around them. Of course, this is an organic process, and some things you planned will not work exactly like you thought; narrative is part of a global experience and you will have to grapple with other departments (or people) that will directly impact your work. VR, like video games, requires a highly interdisciplinary and iterative approach.

For example, if you create a VR experience with no dialogue because you have neither the budget nor tech for it, or simply because you deliberately choose not to use dialogue, you will have to manage without them to convey your narrative, meaning you will have to think of other ways to deliver information in the story world – maybe, for instance, visual cues and information within the environment will convey most of your narrative. Or, if you decide to set your VR experience in the cabin of Nemo's Nautilus, you will have to build your narrative entirely within this small place; environment or ambient sounds will probably be two of your main narrative means… or not! It is precisely your job to select the narrative elements you think will be the best fit for your story and discuss them with the team to fit with their own constraints.

There are multiple ways of conveying a narrative through a VR experience, and once again, you may have access to only some of them for many different reasons. This is why listing your narrative means should be done in the early stages of the work, depending on inputs from the other departments you may work with. Go into as much detail as possible when listing your narrative tools. For example, if you use dialogue in your experience, specify which kind of dialogue, that is, if they are interactive, in which level are they communicated, etc. The sooner you identify your narrative means, the better your narrative will adjust to the whole experience you are creating.

In any case, constraints are a source of creativity; they force you to think outside of the box. So, if you have to find a way for your character to communicate their feelings without using dialogue, you will surely come up with ideas that would have never emerged without this specific constraint. Consider constraints as creative opportunities.

IMMERSION HAS ITS LIMITS

At the exact time when the user puts on a virtual reality headset, they are literally catapulted into another world. The feeling of being somewhere else, of being physically present in a fictional world, is so powerful that the graphics' degree of realism makes little difference since the space seems *habitable* – meaning the user feels like it is coherent, familiar, and natural. The user is more than willing to accept the new rules of the virtual worlds they are about to dive into. Because strangely, nothing seems *virtual* in VR, at least for new users. This is the power of immersion.

Along this power of immersion lies the power of *illusion*. That is, the moment when the fictional world appears before the eyes of an audience who genuinely believes in its existence, leaving all logic and sense aside. Every medium using innovative technologies possesses this power of illusion for a time, particularly theater (shadow theatre, for example), photography (spirit photography being one of many examples), and cinema (*The Great Train Robbery* and the movies by Méliès – whom we still admire for his art of illusion by editing – are famous examples of this sense of wonder introduced during the early days of the medium).

But as the viewers get used to a new technology, they begin to see behind the curtain, understand the tricks, and learn how the magic happens; thus, the power of illusion starts to decrease if it does not evolve. Nowadays, the power of illusion owned by cinema or theater has not disappeared, but its audience has evolved. A gangster shooting from the screen (as was the case in *The Great Train Robbery* in 1903) will no longer make the crowd shout in fear or run out of the theater anymore.

Virtual reality still fully owns the power of illusion. It will not last. There will be a moment when the curtain falls. To be able to immerse the audience in a fictional world, creators must understand the key components of illusion. One of them is a well-established principle: a fictional world must be consistent in order to stay believable and immersive. As all writers know, a lack of consistency in a fictional world breaks the suspension of disbelief. VR is no exception to the rule. In any case, writers cannot (and should not) rely on technology only to sustain the illusion and support their narrative.

With this in mind, one of the storyteller's first concerns should be the *user's agency*. Game designers know that *player agency* is fundamental when creating a game. It is not just about giving the player the possibility to interact with the world; it is about giving them the ability to make meaningful decisions or actions that will affect the world. For example, players can be asked to make tough choices – such as rescuing or harvesting the Little Sisters in *Bioshock*, or betraying people in *Beholder* or *Papers, please* to protect their family – that immerse them even more into the story world by giving them a real and direct impact on it.

In VR, writers can take a step further and exploit the user's body to increase their feeling of belonging in the fictional world. The user's head movements reproduce how they look at their environment in reality, their hands can be used to interact, or they can even walk in the virtual world as they would on the street. Immersion is always more effective when the user is involved mentally *and* physically, since it is closer to the way they actually perceive the real world on a daily basis.

USERS ARE THE CORE OF ANY VR EXPERIENCE

The question of a player's avatar has largely been discussed in video game studies. When they enter a game, players accept to take control of a character (or characters) and to pretend they are this character. In virtual reality, embodiment is central. When the user enters the virtual world, their body enters with them, and the limits of the space they initially occupied are immediately reshaped. This feeling of belonging to the fictional world is mainly brought on by the annihilation of their immediate surroundings, that is, users are completely cut off from the real world. It is also brought on by the interaction the player has with the virtual world. The fact that their virtual hands are visible in this world (which follows their real movements) creates an emotion specific to VR. So, when the user grabs an object in the virtual world – as long as the physics, haptics, and controls are well-designed – the user feels that the object is really there between their fingers.

If the players are engaged in the virtual world because they have some kind of agency over it, they will likely ask themselves at the beginning of the experience: *Who am I? What am I?* It will surely depend on the impact you allow them to have on the world: the more they feel concerned and directly involved, the more they will engage themselves in the experience.

Obviously, this is still a *roleplay*. As immersive as VR can be, users are still themselves, standing in a room with their headset on. They do not magically become some fictional characters in the middle of a fictional world. However, the user's avatar stands as a major narrative mean, for it allows writers to convey a narrative directly through the user's body – their role inside the experience, interactions they have with the world, and their direct impact on the latter all mean something.

A writer should concern themselves with following critical questions: *Who or what will the user incarnate in this world? What perspective will it give them on the world? What does their avatar look like? Do they have a body, hands, feet, shadow? What agency do they have on the world and how do they interact with it? Can they move things, break things, or perform whatever actions with direct impact? Above all, how will all these decisions eventually support and expand the narrative?*

If you don't give any information to the user on their identity by using body parts, specific perspective, or other clues, the user may think – by default – that they are playing as themselves, or they simply won't ask themselves the question. In *Superhot VR*, the user must concentrate on dodging bullets and killing enemies without thinking about their identity in the universe (they don't have time for that!) until the end of a level where they are asked to shoot themselves in the head. They suddenly leave the white raw universe they had been exploring and are propelled to a more realistic one: a narrow office with the door closed, where they discover their robotic hands, computers, and what appears to be a virtual reality headset hanging above them. The user realizes they are part of a simulation. They will return to this office a few times during the game, until the final level where they are asked, for the last time, to shoot themselves. The storyline behind *Superhot VR* is sparse, but effective. Pointing a gun to our own head in VR is strangely impactful, as our brain perceives it as a true threat of possible harm. Here, the question of the user's identity is simply used as a plot point in an experience that is mostly mechanics-driven, but it also supports the theme (our place in virtual worlds) and enriches the story world.

As another example, in *Wolves in the Walls*, the user embodies a presence only visible to a young girl, Lucy. She is the one who draws them at the beginning of the experience, resulting in them entering her world.

Being Lucy's creation gives the user an immediate connection and intimacy with her, as well as a unique and essential role in the story.

Here is the main thing to remember: when giving the user someone or something specific to incarnate, you give them a place in the world, a unique point of view, and thereby allow them to be fully part of this world. Also, there are many ways you could introduce the user to their avatar (e.g., a simple reflection in the mirror; a photograph; an internal voice; other characters reacting to the user's presence; a specific body part such as a robotic hand; etc.), and it will surely help you convey your narrative... or your mechanics, as they must work together.

A GHOST STORY

Some VR experiences choose to give the user a witness status, an external point of view on the story. That is why they are called *ghost stories*. Being able to see without being seen is such an unusual situation in the real world – the famous power of invisibility everybody has dreamt of at least once – that it can easily evoke strong emotions in users by allowing them, for example, to witness things they are not supposed to. Or it can increase their feelings of being strangers in a new environment, leaving the common world behind them, which is the beginning of many stories if we consider Joseph Campbell's *Hero's Journey* concept. Because even if they do not embody a specific character or entity, users will still be a part of the virtual world in some way.

The video game *Myst* has recently been adapted for VR. In this game, the player can explore the world and manipulate objects – their hands are visible, whereas the rest of their body is not. However, when they walk, the sound of their steps on the floor is audible. These two elements only let the player guess that they embody a human. In the original game from 1993, the player's character is unnamed and doesn't have any storyline. The VR adaptation gives the user just enough information to know they are playing a fictionalized version of themselves in this world, and not a defined character. It increases the feeling of discovery and the mysteries floating around *Myst*'s land, as if the player was the survivor of a vessel stranded on the island shores.

In *Down the Rabbit Hole*, the user is also external to the story, as they can switch between two points of view: a third-person POV (or dollhouse view) where they can see the entire rabbit hole's corridors and move around easily, and a closer third-person POV allowing them to control Alice from inside the rabbit hole. Both views must be used to discover clues and progress the story, since some details cannot be seen without doing so. Here, the main character is Alice, whom the user does not embody. Designers probably wanted to explore classic game mechanics in a VR environment rather than to work on the user's role inside the story.

Once again, choosing the user's point(s) of view is up to you and your team and must serve your story. Remember: they are key to the user's global experience and, therefore, an essential part of your work on narrative.

KNOW THE LIMITS OF YOUR GENRE

The feeling of standing in the middle of ancient ruins, floating in a spaceship above Earth, or running on a battlefield is always impactful. But encounters with characters in VR are also fascinating and serve as a powerful tool for writers. Some experiences allow users to approach characters closely (or characters to approach users…) to the point where they can almost smell their breath. With no frontier between the user and the fictional content, this can be a highly efficient tool to trigger emotions.

In that sense, horror in VR is the best example. The feeling of being physically present in the fictional world, together with the presence of threatening characters, can be deeply disturbing. It goes without saying that moments of horror should be used with caution: if your goal is not to frighten users, think twice before making a character suddenly appear in a dead angle! Non-horror experiences can easily become oppressive and jarring unintentionally, so this is something you should take into account when writing your scenes.

ENVIRONMENT AS A NARRATIVE PILLAR

If the user can get close to the characters, they can also get close to the settings. Here enters environmental storytelling, a major tool for game designers that also heavily applies to VR.

Environmental storytelling is the art of delivering pieces of information about the world, characters, or story in the environment, whether through macro-elements (e.g., buildings destroyed by bombs and other visual information that indicates the user is in a war zone) or microelements (e.g., a family painting in a manor and others visual cues that indicate the woman who owns the manor is no longer married). Each element, be it macro or micro, just by its mere presence, delivers information of the world or character that adds to or sheds light on the game's narrative. Environmental storytelling should make the player feel: like they are wandering a living world with a past, a present, and a future; and—if the user is meant to be active in the experience— that they will have an impact on this future.

In video games, depending on the way designers have chosen to control the flow of narrative information, players will discover information in a given order and in different forms. The environment they find themselves in is one of the ways to convey that narrative information. One of the most effective examples of this was in *Little Nightmares 2*, where the environment delivered crucial context and foreshadowing opportunities in a single exterior image: a rope is hanging through a school's window, evoking the attempted escape of children and preparing the player for the scary characters they will encounter inside. In a way, environment storytelling is about telling little stories that will progressively form a web, that is, the macro story of the fictional world.

In his article "Game Design as Narrative Architecture," Henry Jenkins calls these elements *micronarratives*.[3] He makes a valuable link between environmental storytelling in video games and Disney's amusement parks by quoting Don Carson, a former Senior Show Designer for Walt Disney Imagineering:

> "The story element is infused into the physical space a guest walks or rides through. It is the physical space that does much of the work of conveying the story the designers are trying to tell... Armed only with their own knowledge of the world, and those visions collected from movies and books, the audience is ripe to be dropped into your adventure. The trick is to play on those memories and expectations to heighten the thrill of venturing into your created universe."[4]

In VR, like in video games or amusement parks, environment is one of the major components of immersion. The users are hungry for details delivered through environment mostly because, in VR, they often have time to observe and get very close to settings. Realism doesn't matter here: realistic environments such as the ones from *Half Life: Alyx* or unrealistic ones such as *Job Simulator* are both as immersive. One of the reasons for that is they both use meaningful details rewarding an attentive observer, be it a toilet door marked "Humans" in *Job Simulator* or two skeletons sitting close together on a couch like lovers in *Half Life: Alyx*.

---

[3] Jenkins, Henry. "Game Design as Narrative Architecture." Henry Jenkins' Blog, 2004. http://web.mit.edu/~21fms/People/henry3/games&narrative.html

[4] Ibid

In the documentary *The Imagineering Story*,[5] Disney imagineer Coulter Winn talks about the four different levels of details in settings Walt Disney advised his team to build upon. This is great advice for VR writers also:

Level 1: You're in the country, you see over the trees some tall buildings, maybe a church steeple.

Level 2: You've walked into town, now you're on Main Street.

Level 3: You're looking closely at the colors and texture of the buildings.

Level 4: You've gone up to the front door and you're grabbing the handle, feeling the texture and temperature of the material.

However, the goal here is not to overwhelm the user with details. Details are only interesting when they support the world and story. Putting a virtual reality headset is like falling into the rabbit hole: make the user feel like the world they wander is real, until they find a way out and realize it was just a dream… and wish they had never woken up.

LOCOMOTION IN VR

Allowing the user to explore their virtual world seems like a wonderful perspective for writers. But when it comes to locomotion, things can get complicated.

The smallest recommended area for VR users is 6.5 feet by 6.5 feet, and most of them do not have a larger space. Because VR is mainly used at home, designers must think about ways to let the user move within this small space, using trackpads, thumbsticks, or other walking-in-place methods. However, smooth locomotion, teleportation, or any kind of artificial movement in the virtual world will eventually cause discomfort and motion sickness. And depending on the kind of experience you are designing, this may affect the believability of your world and, therefore, immersion. If possible, try to incorporate the locomotion method to your narrative, just like you would with a game mechanic.

DRIVING THE USER'S GAZE

Screenwriters (when they do not direct the movies they write) know that shot indications or anything that lies within the director's job must not

⁵ *The Imagineering Story*. Directed by Leslie Iwerks, performance by Angela Bassett, Iwerks & Co., 2019. Disney+, https://www.disneyplus.com/series/wp/6ryoXv1e1rWW.

appear in the script. Screenwriters are expected to write the story and leave the rest to the film crew as long as it does not impact the story – shots, editing, settings details, costumes, etc. This is different for VR, where writers must think about the experience as a whole, at 360°, as precisely as possible. Staging is part of the writing. Writers must consider what happens in front of the user, behind them, on the sides, above and under, at every step of their progression, taking into account their POV (*point of view*) and FOV (*field of view*) and which pieces of information they will eventually miss in the process. That is why VR designers sometimes use dollhouse views (top-down views) to navigate into the virtual space and work on the user's progression. (*Job Simulator* offers this dollhouse view as a reward when you complete a level, if you are curious about what it looks like.) Dividing the script into four parts per sequence (front, back, left, right) is also a solution to visualize the story; it allows the reader to understand what is happening for simultaneous actions. There are no rules when it comes to writing for VR.

As an example, a VR screenplay can resemble a movie script, where the actions would be divided in FRONT (the first thing the user will see), BEHIND, LEFT SIDE, and RIGHT SIDE with a description of the settings at the beginning of the scene.

INT. SPACESHIP CORRIDOR — NIGHT

We are in the middle of the spaceship's corridor, in darkness. Hard to see anything.

FRONT. *Trigger.* A light suddenly turns on in the distance. Footsteps. Someone is coming from there.

BEHIND. The light reveals a door. It is closed.

LEFT SIDE. A window lets us see the surface of Mars. The spaceship is moving fast toward it.

RIGHT SIDE. In darkness.

Triggers are useful to sequence the major beats of the experience. For example, the user entering a room will trigger an alarm. Or a specific line of dialogue will trigger a fight. Et cetera, et cetera. If information is essential to the overall narrative progression, you might think of a way to trigger its appearance (be it visual or audio) by way of a specific action from the user. In that case, they will not miss it.

You can also drive the user's gaze by using visual or sound stimuli. If the user hears footsteps behind them (thanks to binaural sound, which is 3D stereo sound), there is a great chance they will turn around to see what is coming to them. Or a light in the sky will likely make them look upward. Some experiences also use this user's gaze to trigger events, meaning that if the user does not look in a certain direction at a certain time, nothing will happen.

Never forget that users will not always act as you planned. If you build an entire scene thinking they will follow, without fail, all of your visual and sound stimuli, the scene may not work. Once you defined which elements of information the user should not miss, select the most effective tools to guide them on the narrative path(s) you built for them. It could be a visual or sound stimulus that will create a feeling of urgency to optimize the chances that the user will follow the action. Once again, sequencing these actions will help you control the pacing of user's progression in the experience and prevent them from missing important story beats. Also, consider using sound when you can and when it is relevant; if the user fails to see the rocket lifting off, they will surely hear the blast of the reactors.

THE QUESTION OF INTERFACE AND TRANSITIONS

Since VR allows users to interact directly with a virtual world, anything standing between them and this world is at risk of breaking the immersion. Editing or interfaces can, therefore, become an issue.

Traditional shot transitions (such as a *cut*, a *fade to black*, or a *fade in/ fade out*) do not usually work that well in VR. Finding ways to avoid them is part of your job since it should ideally be embedded in the narrative. You could use parts of the settings and transform them into something else to introduce the next scene, like a scene change in theater. Or you could drive the user's gaze upon a specific element, say, a character in movement, who will lead them to a different setting and timeline, like in *Gloomy Eyes*.

The same thinking must be done for the interface or any on-screen texts. In video games, designers decide either to use a HUD (heads-up-display) to show information on the screen or do without it. In VR, using a HUD is often a technical nightmare, mainly because there are no screen corners. In case you need an interface or text such as subtitles, as for locomotion, you might think about ways to incorporate them within the story world – just like *Half Life: Alyx* did, where the character's health is displayed directly on his robotic hand.

DIRECT ENVIRONMENT AND COLLECTIVE EXPERIENCE

Most of the time, virtual reality is a solo experience. Users are alone in the virtual world, and even if they can sometimes interact online with others, they remain alone in their room. But there are also collective experiences (called LBE, or *Location Based Entertainment*) happening in public places, where the natural sensorial elements of the physical environment enhance the VR experience.

LBE VR gives the writer extra tools. Here again, you have to ask yourself why your VR experience must be designed for multiple users gathered in the same room. What exactly will they share? Do they see each other in the virtual world? Do they have to cooperate using the same physical space? Do they hear the same sounds? What are you trying to make them feel as a group?

The actual physical space hosting the experience can be used as the foundation of an immersive digital environment. Imagine the writing possibilities. Users all gather around a physical table and put their headsets on. They enter the virtual setting, say, of the interior of a futuristic spaceship. Each of them now embodies a different character sitting at this table and sees the others as their avatars. Settings, actors to portray some characters, and even temperature and smells from the physical world can support the immersion. The users share the same experience, but at one point, each of them will witness a unique scene with their own character. Therefore, they will gather information on the plot that no one else knows about... until the end of the experience, when they will discuss what they have experienced individually and will gather different pieces of information to understand the plot as a whole. (In transmedia storytelling, game designer Neil Young tells media scholar Henry Jenkins that he refers to this as *additive comprehension*.)[6] In order to create a rewarding collective experience, you also have to think about the individual experience, mainly how much can be personalized per player and when to dovetail back to the collective experience.

EXTEND YOUR SKILLS AS A WRITER

VR storytelling is about narrative *and* design. As such, learning the rules of storytelling is as important as learning the rules of interactivity. Roughly put: what does it mean to deliver your story in an interactive environment?

---

[6] Jenkins, Henry. *Convergence Culture: Where Old and New Media Collide.* (New York: New York University Press, 2008).

This is something writers coming from cinema or theater will have to learn, while video game writers will probably be better equipped to tackle the challenge. One thing is for sure: VR needs writers and designers who can master multiple tools in order to convey a narrative that comes with specific constraints.

Writing for VR also requires a deep understanding of collaborative creation and, by extension, the need for iteration. For writers who are used to working alone, this is a major skill to learn. Your narrative will be deeply impacted by the work of other departments. So, you will have to adapt mainly by understanding the skills and contributions of your collaborators, how their expertise can help you convey your narrative, and how your expertise can help their craft. One of the unique requirements of interactive writing is that you write *and* design the narrative experience. It is a highly transversal craft.

Users still have to adopt this new technology that is VR, so writers and narrative designers will have time to test and learn. As we say in the field: You have to do your craft!

REFERENCES

Books

Jenkins, Henry. *Convergence Culture: Where Old and New Media Collide*. New York University Press, 2008.

Manovitch, Lev. *The Language of New Media*. MIT Press, 2001.

Film

The Imagineering Story. Directed by Leslie Iwerks, performance by Angela Bassett, Iwerks & Co., 2019. Disney+, https://www.disneyplus.com/series/wp/6ryoXv1e1rWW.

Online

Jenkins, Henry. "Game Design as Narrative Architecture." Henry Jenkins' Blog, 2004. http://web.mit.edu/~21fms/People/henry3/games&narrative.html.

CHAPTER 4

Building Narrative in Mobile Games

Bay Anapol

CONTENTS

IN THE FALL OF 2011, I headed off for my first day as the primary game writer on Microsoft's ambitious *Project Spark* – armed only with a giant backpack, my precious lanyard pass, and a passionate love for well-written console franchises like *Ratchet & Clank*, *God of War*, and *Fable*. I soon learned that the company's "Bldg C" was a labyrinth of such hobbit-like proportions that it was possible to forget where your desk was on the way back from the restroom (this happened to me an embarrassing number of times), that it was wise to avoid on-campus dining at noon, that one's career path is never a straight line, and that even great teams can end up with canceled games. This is all to say that despite everyone's best efforts, *Project Spark* sadly ground to a halt 2 years later, and I never wrote another console game. I've designed mobile game narratives ever since.

DOI: 10.1201/9781003141594-5

While I enjoyed my time at Microsoft (and remain close to many of my original team members), I have no regrets leaving console development behind. Mobile is a good fit for those who prefer a faster pace, better work/life balance, and quick creative pivots. And although it lacks a bit in perceived glamour (and it is admittedly rare for anyone to point out great narrative turns, in, say, *Candy Crush Friends*), my role as a mobile games vs. console games narrative designer is not all that different. Game narrative – no matter what the medium – exists to make gameplay more addictive. This is always the goal. The variations are a little more subtle:

Console Game Narrative Design	Mobile Game Narrative Design
More leisurely ability to tell a story with cut scenes and in-game nonplayable character ("NPC") dialogue to create character development.	Narrative wrapper happens in very short spurts, often with scrolling text.
"Movie"-style moments allow the player to see the characters out of gameplay.	Characters are developed via bite-sized content, delivered carefully around gameplay.
The player experiences longer play sessions with more room to introduce narrative concepts as well as gameplay segments.	Short play sessions leading to less ability to remember small narrative turns.
Characters can be introduced into the narrative, disappear, and reappear later.	Characters are less likely to be remembered after many hours of short play sessions.
Typically, a high budget for animation and voice-over acting – often performed by Hollywood actors.	Lower budget, less animation, and a player less likely to play with sound at all.
Players pay a set amount to experience the game, with "completionist"-style players completing all side quests and Easter eggs.	Players are offered the option to pay for boosts and vanity items, and may choose to skip side areas entirely to use items on the main narrative and gameplay flow.

While narrative design is a hugely important component to a successful game, it is still often one of the last positions hired on the team (and that's if there's room in the budget, or the developer suddenly notices that the text sounds like "all your base belong to us," a 1991 example of what not to do in game writing and localization, thanks to the poorly translated Japanese game *Zero Wing*). I once had a producer ask my help in hiring a narrative designer because their game needed "words and things." This is a little like hiring a pilot because you need someone to name the controls. Narrative designers *do* write text, but they should play a more important role. By creating a world, narrative design creates engagement ("I like this world and the inhabitants"), decreases the friction that causes players to quit a game ("I don't understand what I'm doing"), increases immersion ("I don't want to leave this world, even though dinner is ready!"), and gives play meaning ("I understand why I'm inside this world."). Narrative design clarifies the goals of the player and helps them understand what they need to do to be successful. But perhaps most importantly, without narrative, the world is not only empty of characters and items. It is empty of meaning and human connection.

I find the search for meaning is one lesson I've taken from writing fiction to writing games. A great writing teacher I studied with in graduate school told us this and I never forgot it: "You have to find the love in a story." She didn't mean romantic love or even actual love between characters. She meant humanity. I still do this in my game writing. I try for relationships that feel organic and human, and characters who feel true and resonant. Ultimately, these reverberate and bring players back to your game. The other lesson I bring from my fiction background is that it feeds your work to read everything, and I mean everything. Read Dickens. Read Jane Austen. Read Dostoyevsky. Read Shakespeare and Phillip K. Dick and Ursula K. Le Guin and Isaac Asimov. Read Chekhov. Figure out how they plot and how they make you care about the people and situations in their books. Of course, playing games is important, and as a game narrative designer, I expect you'll play the great games as well. But reading is fundamental to writing, and writing is your medium as an artist. I'm not exaggerating when I say that I've picked up novels like *The Great Gatsby* (which is nearly perfect in every way) to help me figure out problems in branching narrative or character development. (I'm certain that F. Scott Fitzgerald would have been a great game writer.) So going back to the classics for inspiration is one of the best lessons I can impart.

Speaking of lessons, I can sum up my wisdom about Narrative Design in 6 bullet points:

- There can be only one vision holder for a game. Respect that even when you disagree.

- Narrative's value is in helping players both embrace and understand the game's goals.

- You are likely *not* the audience. Think like the player.

- Immersion leads to retention+monetization. Try to create an immersive "dream state."

- Games are a visual medium. Don't lean on text alone to create a world.

- Always serve the game first – *not* your particular discipline.

Now let's discuss how it (hopefully) comes together in mobile-based casual games.

CREATING AN IMMERSIVE WORLD

The term "casual game" is inexact at best. It refers to the style of play rather than the mechanic – which can be anything from switch, chain, bubble shooters, Match-3, collapse to merge. Typically, a developer decides on a mechanic before deciding on the "world of the game" around it because this choice doesn't affect the game world as much as, say, first person shooter vs. RPG (although some recent merge games have placed the world on the gameboard so there's no need to toggle back and forth between gameboard and meta-game). The term "free to play" is equally puzzling, as development depends upon players continuing to pay to unlock boosters and clues.

Whatever the mechanic, mobile and casual go together like peanut butter and chocolate (I say this as a peanut butter cup fan). A phone in the pocket means your games are always with you. This strongly influences the type of gameplay and narrative that a player will experience. The play session morphs from long and naturally immersive (a dark room and a headset, for example) to quick and easy (5 minutes parked between school pickup with a toddler in the car seat). This is slightly unfortunate for narrative designers, as the advent of the casual game phenomenon has led to a certain misunderstanding of the role of narrative. Since games don't look like movies in this genre, some developers don't see the need for narrative or design with narrative as a bolted-on overlay and not in tandem. It's too bad since it's a much more cohesive player experience when narrative is developed in lockstep.

In fact, I hear rather often that casual games have no need for narrative (which begs the question: Then why do I have to be in so many meetings?). It's been cheerfully explained by long-standing industry types that, "let's face it, you don't need a story for a Match-3." I would bet that this belief stems from the fact that most people consider narrative to be plot-based and text-told: a traditional story that unfolds sequentially from beginning to end. That's not how casual games tell a story, though. The medium doesn't lend itself to traditional storytelling or a plotted experience. Instead, it's about world creation. This is because console games and casual games are played very differently.

Console games are designed with enough features, complications, and plot dynamics to attract long session/completionist players. Casual (mobile) games are designed for short-spurt players, delivering bite-sized gameplay and narrative replete with simple, understandable goals. A successful casual game allows the player to return to the game (often after days or weeks) and immediately recognize the world and their goals. A well-designed narrative anchors this concept.

Consider your prototypical console player. They might plan their play sessions to give them adequate time. They'll sit down to a few hours of *Red Dead Redemption 2* after dinner, pausing only for a quick bathroom break. Console games are designed for long play sessions. They often tell an unfolding and increasingly complex narrative arc, featuring side quests, multiple characters, and movie-style immersion. Now consider your average casual player. The play session is unplanned because their phone is always in their pocket. They might board a bus for 10 minutes and have enough time to play five levels. At their stop, they'll put the game aside until their evening commute. When they do play, there's usually a lot going on around them. Maybe they're texting at the same time. Maybe they're wondering if they should grab dinner. The game is designed for stop-and-start play, and the narrative reflects this by not insisting they remember too much complexity.

How you communicate your world to the player – or the method of narrative delivery – is also going to be different. Console games can feel like movies, with long and involved cut scenes, and even characters that are sometimes voiced by famous actors. Mobile games do not lend themselves to long cut scenes. After all, a phone has a much smaller screen than a TV connected to an Xbox has. The cut scenes are not only not going to have famous voices (sadly for sound designers, many casual gamers habitually turn the sound off while playing) but are also going to be a lot less polished because the budget is lower – mobile developers are not aiming for the film *Avatar*. Even when developers add cut scenes, they are usually equipped with skip buttons because designers are aware that not every player wants to watch them. Quick pacing is a big consideration in casual games. Cut scenes can slow things down and interrupt gameplay. (I would argue – and I have – that if you must have a skip button anywhere, think about whether you actually need the expensive asset you just invited players to skip.)

Plus, there's no better way to ensure that a player will abandon your game than turgid transitions and long narrative moments that interrupt game flow and make players itch for a skip button.

This doesn't mean that narrative isn't an important driver for casual gameplay. Narrative provides a cognitive reason for WHY players are performing mechanics. It creates characters and situations to root for and help. It puts the player in a "dream state" of an alternate reality – encouraging them to play level after level. This, in turn, leads to retention which leads to monetization because when players invest in a game over the long term, there's a much better chance they'll spend money to enhance their gaming experience.

Spil Games CEO Tung Nguyen-Khac echoed this idea in a 2017 article in Gamesindustry.biz.

> "Narrative has become important in mobile gaming because it
> improves engagement and keeps people coming back to a game.
> Returning players are more likely to spend money, so narrative is
> a way to increase the revenue value of a game."[1]

He was right. Narrative continues to cheaply and effectively brand a game – it's a way to stand out and be recognizable immediately. Creating iconic moments drives players back to a game they feel resonates in a familiar and comforting way. Good, well-placed narrative also adds another well-known driver – players want to find out what happens. Creating cliff-hanger moments is a great way of pulling players past difficult levels.

So narrative is a genuine driver for gameplay, branding, and retention. But how do you create a truly immersive world within the compact space of a phone screen? This is the particular genius of games with what is now known as a **light narrative wrapper**. While I believe that all games *have* narrative (take *Candy Crush*'s iconic crying Tiffi or the feeling of being inside a toy box in *Toy Blast*), *Homescapes* is a good example of this new and more narratively based genre. It removes the saga map that bounces the player up a graph and places the player inside a content-driven world. In other words, familiar gameplay elements (Collapse or Match-3 are the most popular) are "wrapped" in a hopefully addictive bundle of world and character, where progression is scored by the unlocking and development of the meta-game world. The world *is* the progression bar where a player

---

[1] Batchelor, James. "Why Casual Games Need Narrative." Gamesindustry.biz. November 23, 2017. https://www.gamesindustry.biz/articles/2017-11-23-why-casual-games-need-a-narrative.

can quickly note how far along they've gotten while discovering more about the story elements as they go.

These are not strictly narrative story games like *Episodes* or *Choices* where progression is based upon a series of narrative (or design) choices with no actual gameplay. In a light narrative wrapper, the story and characters keep driving the player back to the game board. The game board then drives the player back to visual enhancement (what table looks best in the room?) and narrative progression (what will happen to the characters?). Narrative, progression, and gameplay are tied together. In order to unlock various rooms and stories, players must grind through levels and complete tasks. This style of game allows for much more breadth for narrative design and often utilizes the elements below with great efficiency.

Character Design: *Homescape*'s Austin the Butler is either lovable and relatable or annoying and slightly snarky, depending on who you ask. What's much more important is that he's memorable. Players may be annoyed by his slow clap, but they don't forget it. The character design also gives him aging parents (something the game's demographic likely shares), and a giant old house to remodel (a common aspiration or HGTV wouldn't be hugely popular). Austin is additionally a bit helpless and child-like. This answers another common trope – a character that players enjoy helping.

I often refer to the main character of this style of game as the "follow" character. Players spend the most time with them. It is important to ask yourself: Is this a character players will enjoy following? Do we want to see this world through them? Even more important: Do they appeal to your demographic? Are they memorable enough to create social media moments? Do players want to discuss them with each other? Do players want to help them achieve their goals as well as their own game goals?

Homescapes also does a nice job with secondary characters like Austin's parents. While his father often creates problems for Austin, the love between his parents is heart-warming and happy, and Austin is the admirable child we all aspire to be. We might not aspire to *become* Austin, but his goal is relatable (save his childhood home), and his relationships are close and intimate. The world of the game harkens back to a simpler and more gracious time. It is relaxing and comfortable. This is where the mechanics and gameplay are great spurs to each other.

Using Austin's childhood home and parents as an entry into the game is also a great emotional shorthand. It sets up these relatable goals quickly and coherently. The player not only is immediately informed of their goal – help Austin save his childhood home – they understand why it's important. This spurs the player through levels because they want to find out if Austin (through your help) manages to accomplish this goal. This is a gameplay driver. One grand old franchise, *Angry Birds*, manages to get the player's investment without a single word of text in a similar way. Why are we exploding pigs? They're taking away the eggs (or future chicks)! It's always clear to the player where their empathy should lie. It gives their actions purpose.

I can't stress enough how important it is to use character design and relationships to help the player empathize and care about the game's goals (typically the character's goals as well). Relationship shorthand is very effective and can be harnessed in a number of interesting ways – have they broken up with their boyfriend like Lily in *Lily's Garden*? Lost their home? Looking for a secret from their grandparent's chest? Can you use a ticking clock with time running out as a driver? Do they only have a certain amount of time to renovate/remodel before all is lost? (*Lily's Garden* uses this premise very effectively as well.) Time running out, a plucky character determined to prevail, a son who wants to help his parents – these cliches can be addictive if served up with a fresh approach.

I love what Rebecca Harwick, a *Wooga* lead writer, said about character and narrative in games: "You can't form a relationship with a mechanic the same way you can a character. And it's those relationships that stick in the player's mind even when they're not playing."[2] This is the essence of why narrative can make or break a game in a glutted market. Narrative design forms relationships with characters that reach players. Earn their trust by building out characters in a believable and organic way that will, in turn, spur gameplay and retention.

Meta-Game: *Homescapes* uses a very popular design meta-game. It's a crucial mechanic because, without it, the player has very little agency. They are watching events unfold instead of participating in them. The meta-game – in this case, a slow reveal of connections between the house and grounds and community – as I noted earlier is a progression bar. By adding design elements, the player instantly understands how far they've gotten by how visually complex the landscape becomes. (This is, once again, important to retention, as players tend to feel more invested.)

The meta-game is a terrific narrative tool because it allows for assets that can be tagged with meaning for the player. A birdcage with a tough-talking parrot can create a relationship for a follow character. A kitchen

---

[2] Ibid.

choice can recall delicious cookies baked for the first day of school. This provides needed context for unlocking new areas. It's also connective tissue for growing narrative development. The spare bedroom is fixed up for a new character. What's in there that can be meaningful and interesting? Better yet, who is arriving? Keep in mind that less is more. You don't need to bog down every transaction with giant globs of narrative meaning. Sometimes a potted plant is just a potted plant, and that's okay too.

But don't miss opportunities. Just as in a play or a story, it's easier to reveal character when they have something to react to – be it a person, a pet, or a situation to be overcome. The meta-game is where the magic can happen.

Text (Narrative Rewards): Most game developers insist that players "don't read." What they really mean is a little more complicated. Players don't read when there are giant chunks of text blocking their next Match-3 level. Players don't read when the game asks them to continuously read around tutorials, flashing assets, flavor text (no matter how amusing), and quest text. It's accurate to say that players will start to hate reading text when the text is overwhelming and coming at them in all directions. It's all a matter of balance.

If you're inclined to write long dialogue between characters, be forewarned that this can be tricky for a mobile game. It takes a lot of taps on the screen of one's mobile device for call and response. Players can grow weary of exchanges between even the most beloved characters. You also run the risk of the player skipping valuable bits of gameplay instruction due to eye fatigue. (There's that pesky skip button issue again.) Not to mention, people read at different speeds, and localization of languages can wreak havoc with a build (which is not a slam against hard-working localization experts). For this reason, I try to keep dialogue short and punchy. There should also be variety – two taps for all dialogue passes can get old. Keep in mind as well that there are other places to squeeze in the worldbuilding narrative you need. Reward screens are seldom used but excellent narrative delivery methods. A string of flavor text in this location occurs when the player is most receptive – you've won!

A tappable character (where the taps are elective and not required) is another fun way to deliver story bits. This offers players the opportunity to know characters better if they choose to, and it gives narrative designers the chance to add funny bits without slowing down the main flow or interrupting gameplay. It's a nice immersion technique as well as a sandbox to activate while players are waiting for new lives.

Another technique called branching narrative is starting to pop up more and more in games that are not necessarily narrative in nature, and it presents both opportunities and difficulties. Usually this is presented as a choice. The character might wonder aloud if they should say yes to being asked on a date, for example. This simple mechanism gives the player more feeling of agency over what is happening to a character, so that they feel involved in the narrative as opposed to simply watching it unfold. It's a fun device and one that is cheap and easy for the developer. The difficulty is that branching narrative should be a diamond-shape. In other words, no matter what choice the player makes, the game outcome must be the same or you've started a thousand different paths for developers to manage. It's important to be careful not to lead the player down a path that the game can't deliver on.

Branching narrative is just another way to use narrative as a reward, offering an entertaining bit of character or story (along with boosters and coins) for winning a level or opening a new area. This can be very motivating for players, and it's a device I see more and more in the never narrative wrapper games like *Penny & Flo* (which is the clever interplay of a would-be bride and her wedding planner). It's a very good reason to invest in great character development because it only works if the player cares what happens to the characters and world you create. I like to include these bits in live ops (or live events) because nothing needs to be baked into the main flow of the narrative – it's an easy out if players don't care for a particular turn. Figuring out a pattern of narrative rewards connected to events can be a wonderful retention driver, and it's never too soon in development to start thinking about those features.

TEAMING UP

No matter where you work as a narrative designer, you probably won't dash off some ideas, present them at a meeting with the CEO, fist bump as everyone celebrates your genius, and spend the rest of your time typing witty dialogue and approving art. Let me gently dissuade you of the belief that (A) you're going to have that much power, and (B) it's going to be that easy.

As tough as it is at times to accept, there's a lot of good reasons for this. Even the most surefire game ideas must be vetted by a team because every feature has a cost to the developer. It might be the time and energy of engineering. It might be art or the effort it will take to build assets. There's always a balance between what is perfect and what is acceptable, fast, and affordable. Casual games are usually built in a 2- to 3-year development cycle, and I've never been on a game where there wasn't a push to get it out even faster. Games are built by teams and testing, and it needs to hit all the points, not just narrative ones. The process is give-and-take on all sides.

I'm not suggesting there isn't a lot of room for creativity. But it is often coupled with a desire to mitigate risk. Many casual games are built upon the bones of other, successful games. Once *Gardenscapes* successfully launched, for example, other similar design games followed in its wake. *Matchington Mansion* gave us another "fix up a mansion" theme in an obvious homage, and it's done exceedingly well (as is a more recent entry, *Merge Mansions*). It's common to be handed a familiar theme (your family's home must be saved or renovated) and be asked to give it an interesting and marketable spin. Developers spend a lot of time trying to mirror a hit game's success of characters or theme. Keep in mind that you might be a key creative, but there are a lot of stakeholders in a game studio. They include a creative director, producers, game designers, artists, content developers, engineers, audio engineers, and executives. In other words, your sweet and beloved red-haired character might morph into a sassy brunette because someone likes it better or it will upsell to the player base more effectively.

Choose your battles because the process of game-making is collaborative. While you might have one idea what your character should look like, an art director might have another. Your content designer might love the idea of tasks on Mars, although the game is set in Iowa. Asking for a change or redesign is probably going to take time away from something else. If an asset is missing a key element (and once an artist designed a door asset that was literally missing this – it had no key hole!), you'll need to consider the following before you ask the artist for a redesign: Is it critical to the narrative that a key appears? Or can you easily change it in the narrative to remove the detail from the asset? Narrative is cheap but art is expensive. This is why narrative designers are often asked to bend like a yoga instructor. Flexibility is crucial to success.

My perspective is always that I work not for narrative or production, but for the good of the *game*. A great game requires having a single vision holder among the various stakeholders. Once the vision holder is identified (usually the creative director), remember that it is your job to help achieve *their* vision, not yours. However, a good creative director will always ask for input and ideas from their subject matter experts. Even if you are in the position to make important decisions yourself, remember that decision-making is not dictatorship. Flexibility is your friend. Don't get too attached to your ideas. Think like the player.

While narrative is always in service to the gameplay, gameplay is often at the mercy of tech. You might have a wonderful idea for an asset that spins in the air and lands on the game board beautifully illuminating a narrative concept, but tech is busy perfecting a rocket booster. They can't build your wonderful idea so you have to find another. This is always going to be the right call for production. A game without good gameplay is going to fight an uphill battle to get a playerbase. Narrative's role is to propel the player from level to level, and that is fundamentally how a game can prove the success of a narrative design: does it make gameplay more addictive without calling attention to itself?

It's not just the decision of a team or even the vision holder on what appears in a game. It's also the result of stringent testing. Testing is a wonderful boon for narrative since it allows insight into how players feel about characters and the world. Long-form testing, where developers can watch players literally play the game step-by-step, can reveal narrative dips in logic that bother players or places where the narrative bogs down gameplay. It can also reveal whether players are truly enjoying play sessions and what narrative can do to fix it. I've made a practice of watching all my game's test sessions, and my learnings from them have been invaluable.

One of the best parts of being on a team is learning about other disciplines. No one develops for a game in a vacuum (and if they do, they shouldn't). It's the responsibility of a narrative designer to understand and respect the concerns of other creatives working on a game. There's usually a reason why the art director tells you that a particular animation bit you've come up with won't work the way you want it to work. Being a team player means being flexible (there's that word again) and learning about everything. You may not ever QA (quality assure or test for bugs) a game, but you should know what QA is looking for and how to fix narrative issues efficiently.

PROBLEMS AND SOLUTIONS

The road to a successful game is littered with great intentions, discarded features, and many edited strings of data. Putting the good of the game first often means finding creative ways to get around problems rather than asking for changes. I've run headlong into many issues that are particular to casual games, and I'm certain that every casual narrative designer has faced them too at some point.

Think Global, Not Local: This is a global market, so your game should mirror a global audience. Which is to say that the concerns of a US-based audience might not communicate as well to, say, an Asian audience. Localization is important and underrated. It's not meant to be direct translation – it would be easier and cheaper to use Google Translate if this were the case! Great localization takes an expression or cultural norm from one environment and finds its equivalent expression or cultural norm in another. But this is easier said than done if the game rests upon a different set of norms. Sensitivity to your team – especially if that team is based in another country like Ukraine or Russia or China – is key to a successful working relationship. For example, I worked for a long time with teams based in Beijing, China. They were puzzled at times by American mores and culture. This came up during a brainstorming session at the idea of residents needing to save a bankrupt town. One of my co-workers finally explained to me that this scenario is impossible in China, and they didn't fully understand it – why would a government allow a town to go bankrupt? This told me that even if this were explained in the game, the concept might not work for Chinese players. Some ideas just don't translate well from one region of the world to another. It's best to try and understand your audience as well as dig deep for universal themes. Too many New York jokes may leave your California players feeling left out. Don't break the dream state you've created with questionable premises.

Reducing Cognitive Load: How much cognitive load – be it information and/or sensory processing – can you expect mobile game players to carry? The answer should be: not much. Short play sessions, multiple games, erratic play times, and situational gameplay mean that the player will always need to keep their choices within the boundary of the last moments of gameplay. If you offer too much choice or too much complicating narrative, then you run the risk of overwhelming the player. While I think any rule can be broken if you can make it work, it's better not to give more than three choices for an element or a narrative direction.

I also think of cognitive load as overwhelming the player with narrative connections for every stick or stone found in the world. Some of this is essential but too much will start to seem like a chore. If your character consults tarot cards from their grandfather, an iPad from a favorite friend, a computer taken from an engineering seminar they missed on Thursday, a special stone given to them by their vanished brother, a map from their childhood, a globe wedding present – it's going to feel exhausting. It's necessary to imbue items with importance for the player, but picking how and when is equally as important. In the immortal words of Sigmund Freud, remember that sometimes a cigar is just a cigar.

It's another way to think about your visual storytelling. If a character is usually found in one place, there should be a reason to move them around that is easy for the player to grasp. If a character is warm and loving, a sudden shift in personality will be bewildering to a player, even if you love the idea of your main character heroically diagnosing a friend's brain tumor. Players are far from stupid. Remember that they are visiting the world that you're inhabiting and creating – you are always going to be more intimately familiar with this place. Treat your players as honored guests and don't switch the signage that might strand them.

Manage the Content Treadmill: Games need a lot of content. (They also require a great deal of art, and since it's expensive and time-consuming to create, it's usually a big upside if you can find a way for your narrative to reuse some of it.) Live ops (or updated features and live events for an already released game) is a content treadmill that never slows down. You have to figure that some players will burn through content at a breakneck pace (especially if a star system unlocks content by beating levels). A good developer is prepared for this and has a backlog of levels, narrative, and art in advance. But bear in mind that the emerging game narrative typically also supports and contains side quests in the form of events, competitions, guilds, or even visiting characters.

You might be deep into figuring out the next location, but the next 7 locations must be sketched out in your brain. The world has to be imagined as vast enough to keep players happy for years of gameplay, as well as able to keep the characters connected with each other. A great narrative has a pinball effect – events cause other events to happen. While some games have a team of narrative designers, others hope that a single hire can carry a lot of the load. It's definitely possible to do if you can think in terms of what the player needs to find out daily and what the player will discover a month in advance. It may feel like patting your head and rubbing your stomach, but becoming adept at this kind of multitasking will get you far in both your imagined world and your own career.

Limit Resources, Not Imagination: Personally, I love a problem that needs solving. I'm the kind of person who would relish that part of *Survivor* where the now dingy contestant is handed two sticks and told to make an arrow (although I also really love a hot shower). Having to come up with something viable when it can't be done the easy way is the thing I love best. It really gets my creativity flowing to be forced into a corner. That's when you can rub those two sticks together and make fire.

Project Spark, for example, was an interesting game because the team was building the tech as they created the game itself. This put a lot of obstacles in the way of developing the story because we did not have a way for characters to follow each other. As a result, my lead character Hatch was forced to spend a fair amount of time wandering the landscape and talking to himself. This got old very quickly. I longed to give him a pet to relate to, but the tech wasn't there. Poor Hatch was starting to seem a little crazy voicing only his internal monologue. It occurred to me during sleepless nights trying to solve this problem that this was a world where a pet could be anything. It could be a branch. It could be an acorn. But better yet, it could also be a spark of light because we *did* have the tech to create a light source that would follow Hatch around on his shoulder. Not only did I figure out a way for Hatch to communicate with another character, but I also rather inadvertently tied it together with other elements of the game. The ball of light became Spark, which also became the cursor and which also became the name and emblem of the product.

Don't let yourself be set back by roadblocks or limited resources. Your role offers the unique opportunity to come up with creative solutions. Solving this kind of imaginative puzzle is exactly the fun of working in games. It's still a new medium, and you can help invent it.

IT'S A SMALL WORLD, AFTER ALL

A few words about inclusion and diversity. *Insist upon it.* The point is not applauding politically correct decisions; it is making sure your game identifies and understands the player's perspective and allows them the opportunity to see themselves within that world. It's not only the right thing to do philosophically, but it's also key to players investing in the experience. This doesn't only mean multicultural characters (although these are extremely important). It means all varieties of people and representation, including race, religion, age, sexual orientation, and sexual identity.

It's only recently that all women in video games stopped running through games dressed in tiny miniskirts and crop tops *ala* Lara Croft. This is still the default for many designers. I've had to beg for artists to design female characters who will mirror actual players – plus-sized or pint-sized – and not an exaggerated ideal. Game character sizes should be as varied as in life, so body size is another diversity and inclusivity pain point. I've been forced at times to request art character changes because the produced art is unwittingly offensive. I'll never forget a game I worked on years ago that featured a Jewish lawyer villain, complete with a sweaty forehead, enormous nose, and a plan to hoodwink players. Developers from other cultures are not always aware of cultural stereotypes or how insensitive this can feel for a player. It's your responsibility to persuade them, however. It's not easy to request expensive changes, but I've never shied away from this battle, and I never will.

Along with ethnicity, size, sexual preference, gender, and sexual identity, ageism is a rampant issue. If your player base represents 30- to 50-year-olds, your game world should as well. Ageism is sneaky. It tends to cast all older women characters as wise sages or grandmothers or crones. But characters should be dynamic or romantic or heroic at any age or gender, and this doesn't mean adding a few wrinkles to the art. It means considering how these characters view the world. By the same token, designing multicultural characters does not mean simply painting characters a darker color. It means: adding a framework that supports cultural differences that are not merely visual; and ridding your game of cliche characterizations (I've worked on games where the sole envisioned multicultural character, for example, was the housecleaner). Sometimes it means allowing for the appropriate cultural reaction to a situation, such as how to respond to a patrolling police officer or what to purchase at a bakery. At other times, it means that live ops celebrate holidays beyond Thanksgiving and Christmas. It's always a good idea to think a little deeper. Inclusion and diversity should not be superficial.

In the past ten years, I've witnessed developers taking this concept to heart in new and surprising ways. It's a much better canvas than it used to be. I encourage you to do your part in designing a world framework where diversity – including sexuality, hair, and dress – can feel organic and natural. Games can change the world, so allow a new and better world to emerge with your narrative.

FUTURE THINKING

Given quicksilver nature of social media, an increasing market glut, and increasingly limited powers of concentration, players have become much choosier about which games they download and play. With so many games on the market and no upfront investment with a free-to-play game, it's exceedingly common to get bored, delete, and download another similar game. There are two lessons to be learned here. Since there are so many games with similar mechanics and boosters (remove an element with a hammer, anyone?), the need for differentiators to keep players playing remains critical. Remember: the player has no inborn loyalty to your game. They want to be entertained and they want to make a good investment of their time. You must provide both to keep them in your game.

This is not to say that players who have already invested time and money in a game do not evidence a certain brand loyalty. They'd have to spend a lot of both to get to the same level in a new game. But when it comes to enjoyment, a game can never rest on its laurels. It must *keep* captivating players, keep offering new challenges, and keep deepening immersion. A game that is a year into release must work hard to stay at the top. This is where narrative has gained in power and precedence.

The recent release of *Penny & Flo* from the developers of *Lily's Garden* doubles down on the earlier game's skilled characterization and organically conveys dramatic tension with dual main characters of an audience-friendly wedding planner and would-be bride. As the meta-game amps up, the world reflects character choices like choosing a wedding cake – not simply how a random room will be decorated. At the same time, we're learning that this bride might have cold feet. Upping the narrative ante creates more synergy just as vivid characters increase player interest. Instead of returning to a game to get to level 300, the player returns to find out what's happening to Penny and her friends. This is a trend that is sure to grow.

Fortnite, a giant success by any measure, has held onto market shares by innovating for player engagement (including crossovers with popular sports franchises, live ops which are actually released live, and interesting new areas to explore) and has influenced the casual marketplace as well. It's highly likely that casual mobile games will start to follow this pattern of creating real excitement around new releases. Would players wake up at 2 am to witness an actual in-game wedding? This is a question I'd like the opportunity to ask of casual players.

Despite the challenges of keeping player attention, a difficult to engage playerbase is only good news for narrative. Worldbuilding is regarded as an important piece of the successful game. More and more design style games are leaning upon characters and situations to spur gameplay, leaving a wealth of opportunity for narrative to make inroads.

GETTING THE JOB

When I interview narrative designers, I always ask what games excite them. The answers are usually revealing. Sometimes they'll tell me how much they loved *Prototype*, and why it would make a great mobile game. I had one candidate speak for a full ten minutes about why *Final Fantasy IX* is the greatest game ever made (I'm convinced). Applicants, however, almost never tell me that casual games excite them. If they bring them up, it's usually to tell me about the hours they've spent carefully breaking down the narrative in *Gardenscapes* in a way that sounds like pure tedium. If pressed, they'll reel off the casual games they've played and enjoyed (including a year-long addiction to *Candy Crush*), but they'll rarely tell me what *excites* them about playing these games. The word "ashamed" will creep into the conversation, as in, "I'm not ashamed to tell you that I spent months playing *Kim Kardashian*." In other words, I often get a whiff of "I'd rather be working on the *Halo* franchise, but this is good too!"

I don't want to imply there's anything inherently wrong with preferring console games or that it's a bad thing that the desire to work in games often springs from the fond memory of playing *Left 4 Dead*. I expect budding narrative designers to bring that to their work. But if you can't find something exciting about playing casual games, all the breakdowns in the world won't help you create a great experience. How do you come up with an innovative narrative if you can't point to any game that fires your imagination? It's clear that you will not be the audience for every game you develop. But figuring out not just what makes a narrative flow but what makes a game truly fun and exciting is part of your role. A good narrative designer takes it seriously. Once again, you must think like the player. You must imagine their experience. This is always the tipping point.

Of course, to get to this point you have to actually get an interview, and this is not a slam dunk. I won't sugarcoat it: It's an incredibly difficult task to break into a narrative role in the current industry. Programs like Full Sail University are releasing narrative design graduates yearly. More and more established writers from neighboring media like film or television are attracted to the steady paycheck. Add to the mix experienced narrative designers released from shuffling or closing studios, and it adds up to a glut of talent vying for a scarcity of open jobs.

But if you're determined, there are always avenues. Interning at a big company has a lot of value. It's an open secret that people you've worked with in the past are more likely to reach out in the future when they have openings. (In this way, the musical chairs nature of the industry is a boon.) Meeting and impressing colleagues and interning is a great place to begin.

Another option is to get some freelance credits before attempting to apply for full-time positions. Story narrative games like *Choices* and *Episodes* need a massive amount of content, and they hire multiple freelancers to keep their mill churning. Freelancing is another good way to make connections, if a little worrisome in terms of steady income.

There are those who will tell you to learn coding, make Twine games, or get a first job in QA. While it's great to learn to code, I wouldn't do it at the expense of having time to hone your writing. Plus, I don't know anyone who can take the time to play through Twine levels before the interview process (that's not to say it doesn't happen), and it's even rarer that I've witnessed anyone making it out of QA into a narrative position. Game jobs tend to pigeonhole employees, unfortunately. Mind you, there are exceptions to every rule. In general, I prefer to hire narrative designers who are accomplished writers and have thought deeply about the genre. Be a great writer and a good networker. Become someone people would like to work with, both on a personal level and a professional level. Listen as much as you speak. Don't be a jerk. These are words to live by no matter what you do in life.

If you do get that interview, prepare to be tested, and I mean that literally. More and more game studios are insisting upon writing and content tests that can take multiple hours or even days to complete, and they are often looking for something very specific. This takes some time to work to your advantage, but I've learned to love writing these tests and allowing a studio to figure out if I'm fit. Know your strengths and play to them. I would also urge the following:

- *Read everything.* The world of literature is wider than a game narrative.

- *Play everything.* Know where games are heading and what's been successful.

- *Mind your grammar.* There's no excuse for being sloppy in any field.

- *Mind your manners.* A rep for being difficult or ego-ridden is hard to shake.

- *Aim for greatness.* Why be mediocre?

Most importantly, be flexible. Be understanding. Never stop learning.

Ship it!

I have a screenwriter friend who has earned a glorious living for 20 years writing and doctoring screenplays for some major studios. Unfortunately, not one has ever been produced. Despite the high pay (and a couple of cocktail party invites with Jeff Goldblum and Sarah Jessica Parker), I wouldn't trade my career for theirs. Because one of the most exciting things about game narrative design is actually seeing your vision for characters and world brought to life by artists and game designers. It's still exciting to launch a game and know that I had a hand in creating it. This is even truer with mobile games, where the development time is shorter and multiple games are in the pipeline. I have the opportunity at times to know that I contributed not only to a successful game but also to someone's enjoyment. During COVID when everyone needed distraction, I felt good about adding some joy to what has been a bleak time for so many.

While I still write my own fiction, I consider myself incredibly lucky to work in a field that allows me to tell a story. I love knowing that I'm a portal to the narrative designers of the future who will push the genre even further. I want narrative to push more boundaries than I have been able to push. I also want these expanded boundaries to include more opportunities for growth. There's a lot of imagination afire in a new generation of casual game narrative designers, and I honestly can't wait to see – like a true player and reader – to find out what happens.

REFERENCE

Online

Batchelor, James. "Why Casual Games Need Narrative." Gamesindustry.biz. November 23, 2017. https://www.gamesindustry.biz/articles/2017-11-23-why-casual-games-need-a-narrative.

CHAPTER 5

Storytelling and Board Games

Maurice Suckling

CONTENTS

S TORYTELLING EXTENDS INTO BOARD games, and there takes on numerous forms. At the time of writing (February 2021), Boardgamegeek. com (BGG) shows us 2,849 entries with a "storytelling" tag. The board game world is also a dynamic one. Nearly 7,000 newly published games are entered into the database each year, and this does not represent the entire picture – some games and expansions do not necessarily appear on BGG.[1] Since 1996, the number of board games on BGG has increased each year at an annual average growth rate of around 8.9%. Games with a

---

[1] Data extracted from the BGG website. Data as yet unpublished. Considerable thanks go to Yiyun Chen, a graduate student at Rensselaer Polytechnic Institute for his work extracting this data. Note the data were captured in May 2020, hence the apparent tail off in that year. This is only due to incomplete data for that year at the time of capture.

DOI: 10.1201/9781003141594-6

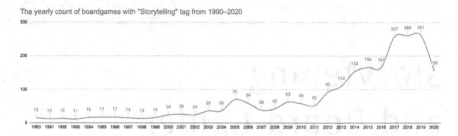

FIGURE 5.1   Annual "storytelling" tagged games growth in BGG database.[2]

"storytelling" tag have also increased. The general trend is an increase in storytelling games, but this is less uniform in terms of its rate in line with non-storytelling games. Nevertheless, the growth is upward since a relative low of 38 games with a "storytelling" tag in 2007. In 2017, there were 257 "storytelling" tagged games; in 2018, there were 260; and in 2019, there were 261. Figure 5.1 shows the overall growth from 1990 onward.

Marco Arnaudo offered up some tools for analysis in his *Storytelling in the Modern Board Game* (2018). These tools help us to identify the means through which storytelling is done in the medium. Arnaudo suggests there are 13 key identifying traits, and where all or most of these are present in a game, we should consider it to be telling a story. He lists these points as:

- A content is present; the game represents something.

- The content is depicted in the components consistently and in some level of detail.

- The rules and mechanics of the game mirror the underlying dynamics of the content they represent.

- Content and mechanics converge in the creation of a consistent imaginary world that acts as the setting of the game experience.

- The events represented in the game are related to one another through a sense of causation.

- The players control individual characters (the traditional focus of storytelling) rather than groups and abstract entities.

---

[2] Ibid. Chart created by Yiyun Chen.

- The players' characters are unique and differ from one another in some significant way.

- An element of identification promotes the formation of an emotional bond between players and characters.

- The players' characters have goals and objectives.

- The players' characters undergo some form of change during gameplay.

- The changing state of the players' characters is a major source of interest.

- The strategies employed by the players mirror the strategies the characters would use in the world of the game.

- The design leaves a degree of uncertainty as to the contents and options that will be available in each game session. A board game would therefore need to mimic some of the sense of progressive revelation that is typical of storytelling.[3]

Further discussion as to what is meant in detail by each trait is best left to Arnaudo. Suffice (perhaps) to say here that Arnaudo gives us a means to move away from an all-encompassing, but ultimately not especially helpful view, that all games are really stories, insofar as there is a story connected to the playing of the game, and perhaps the winning or losing of it. We may agree with most players of games that there are degrees of storytelling happening across the range of board games we now have.

The intention of this chapter is to offer a look at ways (perhaps complementary to Arnaudo's work) in which we might broadly categorize the different kinds of storytelling in board games, with a view to ultimately offering some guidance to writers.

I propose there to be four main categories of storytelling-related board games, with hybrids among them:

- story-making games

- tailored storytelling games

- systemic storytelling games

- other games with narrative elements

---

[3] Arnaudo, Marco. *Storytelling in the Modern Board Game: Narrative Trends from the Late 1960s to Today.* (Jefferson, North Carolina: McFarland and Company, 2018). p.20.

STORY-MAKING GAMES

Example: *Once Upon a Time* (1993 onward).[4]

Narrative Tools: Two decks of cards: story cards and ending cards.

Basic Mechanics: Players have a hand size (of a variable number related to the number of players) of story cards and one ending card. To win, players discard all their story cards by stitching them into an ongoing story, until they only have their ending card, which they play and read out, making it make sense with the story told until that point. There are mechanisms to allow players to interrupt and to take over control of the story.

Example: *The Extraordinary Adventures of Baron Munchausen* (1998).

Narrative Tools: Tokens.

Basic Mechanics: Players take turns to accept a challenge to tell a tall tale in character. Other players may place a token to bet that the speaking character can't incorporate their additional challenge. The speaking character may accept the bet and bring the token into their own pile, or refuse it, by using one of their own tokens. This betting and refusal may continue until players expend all of their tokens. When everyone has spoken, they award all their tokens to the person they think told the best tale. The person with the most tokens at the end is the winner.

Example: *Rory's Story Cubes* (2005 onwards).

Narrative Tools: Customized six-sided dice with a variety of icons.

Basic Mechanics: Players roll the dice and use the icons to construct their own stories, perhaps collaboratively – the "Story Cubes" are essentially a tool for players to use as they see fit.

Some of these games don't actually have a board, yet since BGG lists some without, it seems consistent to include board-less games here too. There is a broad overlap with what BGG tags under the "Story Creation" mechanism family, and certainly with the definition behind this grouping: "Games where you make a story vs. discovering an already existing one."[5]

These games may be driven by players acquiring/being awarded points for their stories, perhaps through collective voting, such as in *Baron Munchausen*, or through the votes of a judge (a player who is not playing in the current round), as in *Kishotenketsu* (2021).[6] These "story-making" games are structured on an explicit or, at the very least, an implicit

---

[4] All game references come from Boardgamegeek.com, unless otherwise stated.

[5] https://boardgamegeek.com/boardgamefamily/65322/mechanism-story-creation

[6] https://steamcommunity.com/sharedfiles/filedetails/?id=2370080053

expression of narrative structure – with reversals or revelations usually forming hinge points for scoring, or are key structural elements of the game design. These games may be driven by players attempting to play an ending card before other players, such as in *Once Upon a Time*. Some of these games may not actually be scored at all, such as in *Untold Adventures Await* (2017). The board, cards, dice, or game systems generate cues for players that are designed to facilitate the creation of stories, which is the central experiential concern of the game. The storytelling load is mostly carried by the players themselves, leveraging the game systems and mechanisms designed to scaffold the story for the players. These games usually prescribe a structure, either through the turn sequence structure (or the fluidity of it), or through the predefined design elements set out for players to define by specific content.

TAILORED STORYTELLING GAMES

Example: *Sherlock Holmes: Consulting Detective* (1982).

Narrative Tools: Booklets, directories, a stylized design-treated map of London, stylized design-treated newspapers.

Basic Mechanics: Players read an introduction to a pre-written/designed case, and then decide which places on the map they would like to go. They cross reference this location in the case file booklet to see if the place features in the story. If it does, they read the text and consider its value on the current case, then decide where to go next. Play ends when players decide they have learnt enough and wish to attempt the questions at the back of the case file booklet.

Example: *The Legacy of Dragonholt* (2017).

Narrative Tools: Booklets with player choices, character sheets, maps, envelopes, other paper props, cards, tokens, dice.

Basic Mechanics: Players create characters, then take them on a series of pre-written/designed adventures, making choices at the end of sections of text as they go, moving to different paragraphs in accordance with those choices.

Example: *Gloomhaven* (2017).

Narrative Tools: Booklets, cards, character sheets, tokens, miniatures, boards, stickers, dials, dice.

Basic Mechanics: Players create characters, then take them on a series of pre-written/designed adventures, unlocking a series of expanding options, transforming the playable storyworld.

These are games where specific paths of pre-written content exist for players to experience. Not all the paths might be chosen and experienced. There is usually a large amount of text to engage with. The experience is often not designed to be replayable in the usual way we expect a game to be. Certain choices will always result in the same specific outcome. The plot underlying the experience is preset – it's already been tailored; although different aspects of it might be experienced in different ways, or different sequences, the material itself isn't reconfigured and doesn't inherently change between replays. This kind of experience is possible once we allow for board games to not be replayable. It is perhaps no accident that the evolution of this game type appears to come, at least in part, through a series like the paragraph choice gamebooks such as *The Warlock of Firetop Mountain* (1982) from *The Fighting Fantasy* series. These "gamebooks" also have no board, although a map is usually generated by players as they play. We have long been accustomed to books not being "repeatable" insofar as they give us no inherently different material each time. Perhaps these types of books contributed to a realignment of our expectations about board games.

SYSTEMIC STORYTELLING GAMES

Example: *The Lord of the Rings* (2000).

Narrative Tools: Board, cards, miniatures/standees, tokens, customized die.

Basic Mechanics: Players use their hand of cards to cooperatively meet a series of challenges, managing their resources to successfully complete the journey to its end, without succumbing to corruption (the power of Sauron).

Example: *Legion of Honor* (2014).

Narrative Tools: Cards, character sheets, tokens, dice.

Basic Mechanics: Players implement the effects of a series of shuffled but still organized cards as they progress through the career of a soldier in the Napoleonic Wars, keeping track of their various statistics to survive (if possible), but mostly to construct a story.

Example: *The Grizzled* (2015).

Narrative Tools: Cards, miniatures/standees, tokens.

Basic Mechanics: Players collaboratively expend their hands of "Problem Cards," pushing their luck to avoid failing in round (by accruing too many matching problems), attempting to avoid too many injuries, and to survive together to the end of the war.

All games are systems of some kind, often housing subsystems within them that interrelate. But describing some games as having a focus on systemic storytelling is intended to distinguish them as games where the story is shaped primarily *through a replayable system*, rather than through the creative work the players do *with the system* (story creation games), or through a tailored story experience. Where a tailored storytelling game usually relies on large amounts of text and has a set plot (which may or may not be fully discovered), systemic storytelling games usually rely on far less text, and rely on systems more complex than essentially narrative choice. Systemic storytelling games usually rely on players making choices between and within intersecting design systems; they rely on managing risk related to resources of some kind. These games also often leverage icons, tracks, or other means of gauging various resource levels. Although these games do not generally offer revisions to their systems between play, and so, in a sense there is no new content, they are designed to be replayable in a way that tailored storytelling games are not. The different choices that players make in their management of the systems, or the different ways in which the systems develop over the course of a game mean that while the same kinds of broad gameplay patterns occur in repeated plays of the same game, they are, at least theoretically, different kinds of game experiences each time. With these kinds of games, there is no plot pre-written, but there is a system pre-designed. That system has its propensities, and these propensities may be discovered by players over time. But in a well-designed system, there is no simple solution which makes replaying the same game a mere repetition working towards the same discovery. In the very least, there is no discovery of a specific underlying plot with the capacity to surprise. In Reiner Knizia's *Lord of the Rings*, the players are always trying to reach Mordor to deposit the Ring, and they are always concerned about having the resources they need for this task whilst avoiding game-ending corruption. In *The Grizzled*, players are always trying to stay alive and survive enough missions to make it through to the end of the war. But in each case, it is the system's capacity to be reconfigured in new permutations that makes the challenge fresh and different for players with different play sessions. The challenge may not always be entirely different, but it is usually different enough in its details that the game is enticing to replay.

OTHER GAMES WITH NARRATIVE ELEMENTS

Example: *Risk* (1959).

Narrative Tools: Board, cards, miniatures, dice.

Basic Mechanics: Move miniatures around a board to battle miniatures controlled by other players to command regions and acquire sets of cards to receive more miniatures to ultimately take over the entire board.

Example: *Twilight Struggle* (2005).

Narrative Tools: Board, cards, tokens, die.

Basic Mechanics: Play cards from your hand to allow you to place tokens on a board representing the world during the Cold War, or to in some other way influence the state of the board or your opponent's ability to play cards to ultimately score the most points by the end of the game, avoiding the automatic loss conditions.

Example: *The War of the Ring* (2012).

Narrative Tools: Board, cards, miniatures, tokens, dice.

Basic Mechanics: In the world of *The Lord of the Rings*, players use dice and cards to marshal their respective forces and use them to secure enough points to win (10 for the Shadow side; 4 for the Free Peoples), while avoiding one of the automatic loss conditions.

These games are systemic storytelling games in some sense, but that aspect is integrated and subsumed within other design/player experience concerns – like being a wargame, or some other kind of strategy game where narrative is deeply enmeshed within the overall experience, perhaps centrally so; however, narrative is of a different quality from an overtly narrative-driven game. In these types of games, the systems are not centrally concerned with close identification of player characters; there is more abstraction in the player agency. These games are not played through the ludic lens of a character or avatar. They do still, however, have some evident narrative elements. Stories are certainly being experienced, with beginnings, middles, and ends, and events occur or are made to happen that resonate as metaphors referring to and analogs of narratives intersecting with history. This is the category to which I would ascribe most – what many would consider to be – wargames. It seems just as wrong to determine that these games are without story, as it is to determine that the story in these games is of the same kind as we see in games with a primary focus on systemic storytelling. Consider: *Legion of Honor,* an RPG-like systemic storytelling game where players have one character and they chart their fortunes through the Napoleonic Wars; or *The Grizzled,* a systemic storytelling game where players have a focus – mostly – on one character in a group of soldiers all attempting to survive World War I. Although these games both have a clear setting in military history, their foci are distinctively different from what we usually find in wargames.

SYSTEMIC/STORY-MAKING HYBRIDS

Example: *Fiasco* (2003).

Narrative Tools: Blank cards, dice (optionally customized or two different colors).

Basic Mechanics: Players collaboratively construct a story using cues generated by the game system, establishing the dynamics between characters, key objects and locations in the story, and dictating the key plot structure. Players then roleplay and improvise their way through this story taking turns to "establish" a scene (deciding on its setting), or to "resolve" it (deciding how it ends). Players use dice to award tokens reflecting favorable or unfavorable outcomes. At the end of the predefined structure, players use their total of different colored dice to inform them how to interpret the endings of their own character's story.

Example: *Microscope* (2011).

Narrative Tools: Blank cards.

Basic Mechanics: Players collaboratively construct a large-scale story together using the game structure to explore and improvise aspects of the story at various levels of detail, moving between narration and roleplaying. There is no winner or loser. The experience is collaborative and ends when players decide to stop telling stories related to the overall key theme or idea together.

Example: *Icarus* (2019).[7]

Narrative Tools: Cards, customized die.

Basic Mechanics: Players collaboratively construct a story of the end of a civilization together using a shuffled but organized deck of cards, using it as a structuring guide for their roleplay and improvisation. Players use die to shape outcomes of player decisions and to add to the tower of dice in the center of the table. Once the tower falls, the civilization ends, as does the game, and players wrap up the story of their civilization's fall.

Some games push the task of content creation substantially on players, but the systems are more complex and refined in the way they do that; these games give players more assistance with carrying that storytelling load, yet they usually accordingly demand more from the players.

---

[7] https://renegadegamestudios.com/icarus-a-storytelling-game-about-how-great-civilizations-fall/

This really may just be a matter of degrees. Just as all games are systems, all story-making games are assuredly systemic too. Nevertheless, I propose some games have more intricate systems than others, and these might be considered hybrids. Analog systemic/story-making hybrid games such as *Fiasco* are sometimes called "storytelling games," or "story games," or "Gamemaster (GM)-less RPG games," or perhaps "indie RPGs." Because these systems are designed to operate without a GM, they usually, by necessity, have some kind of "systemic" design organization that permits roleplaying-like games to function without them. This game type is now really a subgenre in its own right, with active communities and competitions such as Game Chef.[8]

SYSTEMIC/STORY-MAKING/TAILORED HYBRIDS

Example: *Dungeons & Dragon* (1974).

Narrative Tools: Booklets, character sheets, dice. Possibly maps and grids.

Basic Mechanics: Players work their way through a story the Dungeon Master (DM) has created, taking diversions as they choose, causing the DM to create new story matter as required, and work within the game systems (charts, character attributes, dice, etc.) to enact and resolve combat and other actions.

Example: *Tales of the Arabian Nights* (1985 and 2009).

Narrative Tools: Board, book, standees, cards, customized die, tokens.

Basic Mechanics: Players move their avatar standee around the board representing the world in the early Middle Ages, beginning in the center of the board in Baghdad. The avatars embark upon a series of quests in order to win Story or Destiny points. The first player to achieve their target number of both these kinds of points and return to Baghdad is the winner. Quests frequently involve reading from a large book of paragraph-long sections offering choices, then making choices, and suffering or benefitting from the effects of the choice.

Example: *Fog of Love* (2017).

Narrative Tools: Board, card, tokens.

Basic Mechanics: Players collaboratively work their way toward hidden objectives by improvising roleplay around predefined scenario set ups and parameters. Cards are drawn to shape story elements, and tokens are

---

[8] https://forums.gauntlet-rpg.com/search?q=game+chef

placed on the board to keep track of achievements in relation to ongoing objectives.

Some games blend more complex systems (metrics to gauge and cross refer) with a substantial responsibility, for the story's creation itself falls on the shoulders of the players, together with a certain amount of pre-scripted narrative content that isn't intended to be repeatable. RPGs are a good example of this type of storytelling. *Tales of the Arabian Nights* combines the paragraph choice of tailored storytelling with the victory conditions we're accustomed to seeing in systemic storytelling designs, but really calls on players to invest in a certain amount of roleplaying in order to experience the game to its fullest extent. *Fog of Love* has players roleplaying their way through specific scenarios as they monitor specific metrics on their way to a conclusion.

SYSTEMIC/OTHER/TAILORED HYBRIDS

Example: *Risk Legacy* (2011).

Narrative Tools: Board, cards, miniatures, dice, stickers.

Basic Mechanics: See *Risk*. In addition, the board and the available miniatures and cards are modified through the course of play, so a subsequent game on the same board will be different depending on how players have played the preceding game.

Example: *Pandemic Legacy: Season 1* (2015).

Narrative Tools: Board, cards, miniatures, stickers.

Basic Mechanics: Players work together to prevent outbreaks of different diseases from becoming pandemics. Players use their limited actions and abilities to remove infection tokens from the board, representing the world, and to find cures to ongoing outbreaks. In this legacy version of the original base game (2008), the board, cards, and miniatures are modified or added to in relation to each play of the game, building toward an overall layered narrative derived from the game system.

The original *Pandemic* (2008) is an example of a systemic storytelling game. There is narrative, but the system is driving it. *Risk* is a strategy game, where narrative is even more nested within the design, yet still clearly detectable in some sense, yet not through the lens of characters. It's a light, abstract wargame. But when these games are redesigned in "legacy" form, they change in some significant respects. Legacy games are designed with systems where at least some elements are essentially irreversible. Sealed boxes are opened, cards are torn up, stickers are applied to the board, metaphorical doors are shut, and others are opened. In this regard, Legacy games take on an aspect of tailored storytelling games. What is experienced cannot be re-experienced again in quite the same way – at least not without a new copy of the game, and even then, the systemic element of the game won't necessarily give you the same outcomes in the same precise ways.

FURTHER DISCUSSION AND GUIDANCE FOR WRITERS

By way of this chapter's organization, one hopes that there is some clarity that storytelling in board games isn't one homogenous medium. Rather, it is a heterogeneity of often closely aligned, sometimes hybridized mediums that might be grouped under one heading for the purposes of discussion, but this masks a great deal of divergence with regards to specific manifestations of game and story designs. At a certain point, it becomes impossible to say anything of value without taking a more detailed look at the specific designs in question. If we were to attempt to make broad orienting statements for prospective writers in this field, we might allow the following:

1. The tools of the craft most usually feature books, booklets, cards, boards, dice, and tokens of various kinds. Sometimes the tools might also include stickers, or blank cards that players fill out as they play. Sometimes there are customized dice. Sometimes there is software involved, when it comes to hybrid games. Sometimes there are stickers applied to the board and/or cards. Sometimes the only tools are pens and paper, or sometimes even fewer tools than this.

2. There can be similarities with board games stories and video game stories. Both often work in close integration with what may be described as "systems," that is to say, organized structures of networked information – often with their own use of meaningful imagery and frameworks of logic. Where video games also leverage systems related to audio content, this is rarely the case in board games. Board games rarely use sound at all, and when it is applied it is usually as a way of delivering atmosphere. Far more rarely is sound used in more integrated ways. *Juggernaut* (2015) is a rare example of a board game (a card-driven systemic/story-making hybrid game) where sound is used to help with not only atmosphere but also a sense of pacing.[9]

---

[9] https://bullypulpitgames.com/games/juggernaut/

3. The sparsity with which sound is applied in board games is, of course, not the only difference with stories in video games. Systems in board games are often pared back in comparison with their digital cousin. A board game is what Marco Arnaudo calls "... a complex, fragile, and lazy machine – one that performs no work by itself, and that must be constantly solicited by the players through the active manipulation of its physical components."[10] So board games often have fewer systems integrating with other design elements, and those there are often less inherently complex. Even this is a rather broad statement, though, and really needs qualifying by the different kinds of analog or digital games in question. An analog-digital hybrid like *Detective: A Modern Board Game* (2018) shows us that analog elements can be relatively complex. In this case, though, this is in part because of what the digital element in that game facilitates – such as easy and branched access to large amounts of text and more nested revelations through the discovery of more complex clues.

4. Video games have also become extremely adept at teaching players how to play them while in the process of playing them. This is so commonplace today that it almost sounds like a platitude. But bear in mind that this is something board games still have immense difficulty with. There are exceptions. *Mansions of Madness: Second Edition* (2016) teaches players as they play, with the use of an accompanying app. It's perhaps notable that this is another of what we might call "hybrid" games. *Fog of Love* is entirely analog, but has decks constructed within its box so players are taught through the carefully considered instructions baked into the game set up. However, the default expectation is for analog games to still present a barrier to entry as general concepts and rules need to be laid out before playing can begin. Hooray for video reviewers and Let's Play videos!

5. The development process for storytelling in board games is likely to begin with early ideas, brainstorming, and then perhaps some sketches of a board (if there is one), and then details about how systems might work and interrelate. It depends how writers/designers work and the specifics of the project, but once a prototype is designed

---

[10] Arnaudo, p.1.

and playtesting can begin, a cycle of testing and design revisions commence that may culminate in publication (it may never really cease, but publication happens in the midst of this cycle) or culminate in the project being abandoned.

6. It seems far more common that writers simultaneously be designers as well in board game stories. All text can benefit from proofreading and editing, though, and some board game stories are extremely text heavy and do require dedicated writers who might not be closely involved in the creation of the foundational system design creation, but come onto the project with a system "pre-built."

7. Working in board games can suit auteurs, especially in smaller publications, or with more prominent writers. But there is much to be gained from collaboration with artists and publishers. If the game exists within a series, writers/designers can also effectively be collaborating with previous writers/designers even if they never meet or communicate directly.

8. Practical and engineering considerations abound. Budget, board size, card size, how many cards in a deck (beyond a certain number the decks are unwieldy, especially if they are to be shuffled), the number of pieces, the size of pieces, where everything would go on a table so everything fits and there's enough space for people around the edges. There is some give, and some board games have a large "footprint" and aren't unduly criticized for that. Players don't necessarily want lots of pieces. Publishers don't necessarily want only a few pieces. It depends on the game. It depends on the needs of the design. It depends on the appetite of the audience.

9. Success of a story in a board game means different things depending on the type of game. A poor story in a story-making game might not be the result of poor design, but poor playing of the design. In truth, success is a matter of matching the delivered game experience with player expectations. None of this is different from any other product in any other medium. But a perpetual concern highly distinctive in board game stories is a consideration of the relationship between mechanics and theme. Briefly put, a theme is what you are trying to say in relation to the topic you are trying to address (a viewpoint, or set of – perhaps even competing – viewpoints on a topic) and the agency you are affording players to engage with that topic.

The mechanics are the means through which you, as a designer, allow and encourage players to affect and respond to systems within the design – the things you let players do and the impact these things have on the system. Where theme and mechanics support each other, games can be considered successful; where they pull in different directions or seem disconnected, games can be felt to be a failure.

10. Common pitfalls working in this space for a writer include keeping word counts down while working within available real estate, like cards, boards, or player mats. Even if the text is in book form, there can be issues when writing to retain player engagement. So, no waffling or being repetitive. Rules need to be clear. This may be rather obvious, but can be easier said than done. There are many potential pitfalls in a board game design in general, but to outline just two of the more common ones: theme and mechanics not working together (briefly mentioned above), and inactive players (that is, players disengaging while waiting for their turn, or waiting for other players to complete a phase so everyone can move to a new phase). These are, potentially, nontrivial problems.

11. When we consider designing with social responsibility in mind, a major issue is never losing sight of who you are designing for. This requires one to make designs and stories appropriate for the intended age groups of the game, which include artwork and pieces (their sizes and materials) that avoid offense, choking hazards, and so forth. Equally important, but sometimes harder to address, is considering the unconscious biases you're working with as a designer. If you know what you're doing, and why, and for whom, that's one thing. But an unconscious bias might have you ascribe far less agency in your story than might be justifiable from a broader, better-informed perspective. At a more granular level, designers should be cognizant of color blindness in their use of color coding, which can render a game unplayable for some.

12. In the future, I think we can expect to see an increased breadth of topics covered, bringing more diverse perspectives to bear, either on familiar themes or new themes themselves. Initiatives like the Zenobia Award, which had its first cohort of applicants in 2021, give us some reasons to think this might come to pass. The Zenobia Award, named after a third century AD Palmyrene queen, encourages game designers to explore subject matter that appeals beyond its

predominantly heterosexual, white male demographic.[11] I think we will see an increase in the cross-pollination of other game types and mechanics, with many experimental hybrid forms. The sustained success of Kickstarter and related platforms for analog games encourages designers and publishers to take risks and try new things.[12] I think we will see more digital/analog hybrids, but not in any way that imperils the growth of purely analog forms. I think we will also see an increase in the number of games that self-tutorialize as they introduce new players, both through digital apps and in purely analog form.

13. For those with an eye to breaking into board games, the advice I can offer is to move quickly from idea to a playable prototype, then playtest. Then playtest until you're happy, applying bigger redesigns and tweaks as you go. It can be good to step away for a while, then come back to the prototype again with a fresher outlook as you playtest some more. When you're happy with something you have, it's time to approach a publisher. But you need the right publisher, so do your due diligence. Don't fire off 100 emails to different publishers you know little about. It's far better to take the time to learn about five publishers who seem potentially suitable, then write to one and wait to hear back before approaching the next. More specifically, for storytelling within board games, I would urge practitioners to consider how their story is best suited to the medium, and to try to make something in this medium that no other mediums can do as well. But, before all of that, the main thing is to PLAY games. The more you play, the more you will see what already exists and what is popular and what sort of games you like. Also, the more you play, the more you will acquire a larger set of design tools, techniques, and references, which will help you be as well informed and flexible as a designer as you can be. In time, you may even start to blend these different techniques drawn from different sources, thus allowing you access to design approaches

---

[11] https://zenobiaaward.org/who-we-are/

[12] This is in contrast with the situation with video games on Kickstarter. In 2015, board games raised $85m globally, rising to $2,337m in 2018. For video games, $42m was raised in 2015 and $352m in 2018. Board games are not only substantially more lucrative in this sector, but in that time-span rose by a factor of 27, while video games rose only by a factor of 8 and yielded 6 times less revenue. *Board Games Market: Global Outlook & Forecast 2019-2024*. Arizton: Advisory & Intelligence, (2019), p.103.

you could not possibly arrive at by not playing enough. So, to design, first play. A lot. Of all kinds. Even things you don't think you will like. Sometimes especially things you know you won't like.

CONCLUSION

Board games are currently still in a growth phase. The number, variety, and quality of games published each year are healthy, and healthier than they have ever been. New concepts, new mechanics, new combinations of mechanics, new topics, new design approaches on existing topics are all up for grabs. Far from sounding the death knell of board games, the ubiquity and cultural dominance of digital technology seem to be contributing to the considerable and sustained rise of board games. A 2019 market report indicated just how buoyant the sector was and what the forecasts were. In 2018, the board games market in North America, the largest region in terms of revenue, was valued at $3.69 billion. It was expected to reach $6.68 billion by 2024, growing at a rate of 10.40% during 2018–2024.[13] These figures, although pre-pandemic, do not seem to be seriously disrupted as of yet. Some board game publishers have indicated to me in private correspondence that sales during the pandemic were not adversely affected, and, indeed, improved on pre-pandemic forecasts.

This medium is not going away, and there are still so many stories to be told, stories that can't be told in other forms, some of them entirely different stories, some of them told by people we're long overdue hearing from.

REFERENCES

Books

Arnaudo, Marco. *Storytelling in the Modern Board Game: Narrative Trends from the Late 1960s to Today*. McFarland and Company, 2018.
Board Games Market: Global Outlook & Forecast 2019–2024. Arizton: Advisory & Intelligence, 2019.

Online

"26 results for 'Game Chef.'" The Gauntlet Forums, https://forums.gauntlet-rpg.com/search?q=game+chef.
"Icarus: A Storytelling Game about How Great Civilizations Fall." Renegade Game Studios, https://renegadegamestudios.com/icarus-a-storytelling-game-about-how-great-civilizations-fall/.

---

[13] Ibid. p.157.

"Juggernaut." Bully Pulpit Games, https://bullypulpitgames.com/games/juggernaut/.

"Kishotenketsu" Steam Community, https://steamcommunity.com/sharedfiles/filedetails/?id=2370080053.

"Mechanism: Story Creation." BoardGameGeek, https://boardgamegeek.com/boardgamefamily/65322/mechanism-story-creation.

"Who We Are." Zenobia Awards, https://zenobiaaward.org/who-we-are/.

CHAPTER 6

Storytelling in Hybrid Games

James Laks

CONTENTS

OVERVIEW

From the synthesis of analog and digital games comes a new frontier of storytelling called "hybrid" games. By introducing digital elements alongside analog game designs, hybrid games create unique storytelling experiences that combine the player-driven nature of an analog game system with the expandability and versatility of a digital medium. This article will examine three such games – *Detective: A Modern Crime Board Game* (2020), *Mansions of Madness 2nd Edition* (2016), and *Chronicles of Crime* (2018) – and will explore how the digital elements incorporated into each game contribute to the game's narrative experience. Across all three games, digital elements prove to be useful in affording player actions and experiences that would not normally be possible in a purely analog format, as well as removing levels of abstraction between the players and their characters, bringing them closer to the base narrative frame of each hybrid game. These hybrid systems can take on many roles, be

DOI: 10.1201/9781003141594-7

it: an **Information Hub** for acquiring and organizing story and game-relevant info; a **Gamemaster**, helping to lighten the rules load for players with self-governing systems that smooth the flow of play and keep players engaged by reducing nonessential tasks; or a combination of the two. There are other roles these systems can inhabit, but these are probably the most relevant to the three games I'll be discussing here. However, despite these common broad strokes, *Detective, Mansions,* and *Chronicles* all take unique approaches to the specific implementation of digital elements, resulting in dramatically different outcomes with regard to the hybrid aspects' influence on player experience.

For the sake of general comprehension, let's go over a few different terms that are going to come up over the course of this chapter. First is the idea of an "analog game" or "analog game system." These are games that primarily function through the use of physical items in the possession of the players; boards, tokens, and cards are all common aspects present in many such games. For most purposes, it's a fancier, more academic way of saying "board game," though I tend to use the term "analog" more since it also applies to games that don't technically have a board. "Analog game systems" are what drive analog games. They're the sets of rules and processes that allow the game to be played, made up of "mechanics," such as rolling dice, playing cards, or other similar parts of a game. These mechanics are described by "informational documentation," or in layman's terms, instruction manuals. These manuals sometimes provide some level of background as to the story of a game (when present), at least enough to put players into the right mindset to experience a game's narrative. Lastly, weaving a story into the game mechanics of a board game is a complex endeavor, but for the sake of this chapter, we'll simplify it by breaking the games down into two halves: a **design/system-focused side** and a **storytelling/narrative-focused side**. The system-focused side, based on what we just discussed, is made up of the parts of the game that the player interacts with to progress the game on a mechanical level – to advance to the next turn, move a monster, etc. The storytelling-focused side consists of the parts of the game aimed primarily at delivering narrative. This most commonly comes in traditional forms such as descriptive text, but as we'll see, the digital aspects of the three games we'll be looking at make great use of other formats like sound and music to help set the tone and deliver the narrative of the game to players. In actuality, these two "sides" are far more interwoven and are often built side-by-side from the ground up when designing a game, but for our purposes, this two-sided model will work just fine.

MECHANICS AND SYSTEMS

Game #1

Detective: A Modern Crime Board Game (Portal Games, 2020).
Designed by Ignacy Trzewiczek; Story by Przemysław Rymer and Jakub Łapot.

Components

- Physical

  - Game board

  - Player markers

  - Character cards

  - Skill and character tokens

  - Case decks

  - Rulebook

- Digital

  - ANTARES database

  - Any internet search engine

Narrative Experience: Players use their deductive skills to engage in a series of whodunnit, howdunnit, and whydunnit cases, piecing together information from evidence descriptions and suspect files to solve the puzzle before time and their character's own overwrought stress catch up to them. *Detective* delivers two stories at once. The first is that of the player characters, hunting down leads and chasing interviews as described on the various case cards included in the game. The second is delivered piecemeal, in incomplete tidbits through the various personnel and background files in the game's online ANTARES crime database, which the players must sift through in order to piece together what exactly happened in the case they're investigating. *Can be played solo or with up to five people.*

Detective, as its name suggests, is a game about modern detectives solving modern crimes. Players take control of individual investigators and work together to solve a case, represented in analog by a series of double-sided cards that contain evidence, witness interviews, crime scene depictions, and other narrative information in a manner that reads more like mystery fiction than game components. *Detective*'s prime hybrid aspect comes in the form of the ANTARES database, an in-universe online criminology tool containing transcripts, records, and an evidence-matching program that facilitates much of the players' research over the course of their case. Players are only allowed to access ANTARES files that the game cards specifically instruct them to access, though they can revisit pages they've already seen for reference. The ANTARES database takes the form of a custom-built website that players access in order to select their case and eventually submit their solutions, acting as an information hub for players. However, during the game session, it primarily serves as a search engine. Its website is full of pre-loaded information about suspects, evidence, and crime scenes relevant to the case, with players only allowed to access new pages when the physical sections of the game tell them to do so.

The digital aspects of *Detective* both enable navigational ease through the systems of the game and facilitate unique thematic mechanics for players to engage with. The ANTARES database provides a thematic structure that reinforces the idea of the players as "modern" detectives by giving them useful information-gathering tools that are widely available in modern crime-fighting, mainly digital filing systems and access to the internet. Gone are the days of searching halls of filing cabinets – now players can have millions of files at their fingertips *instantly*. It also facilitates ease of use for players and increases the speed of play flow, as most modern players are likely to be familiar with digital databases and search engines, more so than they would be with older filing techniques and parsing long documents, as they do in similar analog games like *Sherlock Holmes: Consulting Detective* (1982). Overall, the use of the ANTARES database serves to reassert the focus of the gameplay: *analysis* of the evidence, rather than the act of searching for it. These facets are not just present in the database portion of ANTARES; the evidence matching system, which allows players to enter codes from game cards to create a cross-referenced list of evidence from their case, gives players the opportunity to easily log all of the evidence they find during their investigation, organized automatically in a single location. Once again, these digital tools help direct players toward the idea that rather than spending all of their time finding evidence, it's the analysis of that evidence that is the point of playing *Detective*. Dead ends and red herrings are aplenty, and if players are simply focused on finding as much evidence as they can, they will find themselves lost in a mountain of useless information. However, the digital tools provided by the game help players to analyze what they find so that sheer quantity becomes less important. The ANTARES database also has a secondary function: cost cutting. By providing most of the game's informational documentation for cases in digital form, it significantly cuts down on the amount of packaging and shipping costs for future content. For games like *Detective*, and indeed all three games I discuss here, this extra content is crucial in facilitating players' continued enjoyment of the game, since once they solve a case they cannot play through it again. Easier production means more possible content, which also means players can continue to engage with the game seamlessly and at length after their initial playthrough.

Game #2

Mansions of Madness, 2nd Edition (Fantasy Flight, 2016).
Design and Story by Nikki Valens, Based on Design and Story by Corey Konieczka.

Components

- Physical

  - Rules reference

  - Map tiles

  - Investigator cards and corresponding figures

  - Cards for items, spells, conditions, damage, and horror states

  - Various tokens for map alteration and marking points of interest

  - Dice

  - Monster figures

- Digital

  - *Mansions of Madness* companion app

Narrative Experience: *Mansions* delivers its narrative primarily in smaller chunks through the extensive use of its companion app. The physical pieces of the game primarily serve to facilitate the analog parts of the system-focused side of *Mansions*, with the companion app taking the heaviest share of the load in terms of storytelling. Players are drip-fed information in small chunks as they search points of interest, explore new rooms, and uncover clues regarding the cases they investigate. The companion app also features sound effects and music (something that *Detective* lacked), which contributes to the overall tone of *Mansions'* stories. *Can be played solo or with up to five people.*

In *Mansions*, players once again take on the role of investigators, though this time rather than stepping into the shoes of a modern detective, they take on matters of the eldritch and occult. Investigating one of several cases through the game's physical pieces and companion app, the players explore an in-game house full of puzzles, clues, and eventually monsters as they try to escape with answers and their sanity. While the first edition of *Mansions* was fully analog and required players to take control over every aspect of the game system's operation, the second edition introduces digital elements to further immerse players in the story-scale events of the game; it reduces their responsibility for the operation of the game system and functions in the role of a "gamemaster" or "storyteller." It does so through a free companion app as a storage and delivery device for large amounts of the game's content, including clue and room descriptions, the contents of search tokens, the mechanics of combat, and more.

With the automation of more of the system-focused side of the game, player (not character) agency shifts by allowing the players to focus on the effects of the system rather than its operation. Take, for example, the game's monsters. In a purely analog environment, players would have to check and double check how the designers wanted each monster to behave and perform their own calculations for damage when monsters attack players. After all of that, they would still have to use their investigators to react to those monsters that they just spent all that time operating. *Mansions* automates a lot of this behavior through the companion app. There's no complex cross-referencing, no damage calculations. All of that work is performed by the computer, with the players simply having to put the physical game pieces in a state that matches the app's output. The focus of the game becomes the players' and characters' experience of the system, in a manner similar to the relationship between player and game in a traditional tabletop role-playing game. Importantly, the app provides narrated descriptions of content, further stepping into its game-mastery role as the computer "runs" the game for the players (for the most part). Many of the game's analog elements persist because they are directly related to the agency of the players. For example: barricades exist as physical tokens to be moved by investigators; search tokens are physical pieces on the analog board to represent the physical actions of an investigator's search before the digital gamemaster reveals their contents; monsters are represented by physical miniatures to show their spatial relationship to the investigators on the game board, even while the actual mechanics of combat are digitally computed by the companion app. Additionally, the *Mansions* companion app allows the game to make use of uniquely nonanalog elements, primarily by introducing sound design through music, sound effects, and narration. This adds an additional factor into the immersive environment of *Mansions'* gameplay – it's one thing to see the miniature of a werewolf on the board and roll dice to attack an investigator; it's another to see its snarling portrait and hear its bellowing roar as it swipes at you with its claws. The digital aspects of the game also allow for more involved puzzles. In a purely analog system, many of *Mansions'* puzzles, such as codebreaker or slide puzzles, would be significantly more difficult to implement with any replayability than in their digital forms, due to its ability to randomize codes and scramble images.

Game #3

Chronicles of Crime (Lucky Duck Games, 2018).
Design and Story by David Cicurel.

Components

- Physical

  - Rulebook

  - Evidence board

  - Cards for people, evidence, and special items

  - Location tabs

  - Forensic contact tabs

- Digital

  - *Chronicles of Crime* companion app

Note: the game also allows for the use of virtual reality (VR) glasses/goggles in conjunction with the companion app. This is not required, and they are not included with the base game.

Narrative Experience: Like *Mansions*, the brunt of *Chronicles'* storytelling is performed through the companion app. The physical game box does not contain any specific narrative content, only items with QR codes used to key the item into the app to allow the players to receive the associated narrative information. Also, like *Mansions*, this game has a key method of storytelling that the other two games largely lack: meaningful visuals. *Chronicles* is the only game out of the three discussed in this chapter that allows players to examine the crime scene environment through visual means, rather than through descriptions. *Can be played solo or with up to four people.*

Chronicles' use of digital elements complements *Detective* and *Mansions* well, enacting something akin to a synthesis of the two. *Chronicles* places players in similar shoes to those playing *Detective*, as they play the role of modern detectives (at least in the base game) investigating a series of cases. Like *Detective*, *Chronicles* uses its digital elements to provide evidence, testimonies, and other essential information to the players, but in *Chronicles*, players acquire this information by scanning QR codes on the game pieces with the game's companion app. It uses these digital elements to aid in player ease and game flow, while supplementing player immersion in the story through unique observation mechanics and evolving narrative content via character interviews that change based on what other parts of the case the player has investigated (more on this later). *Chronicle* features a time gate mechanic, though it is fundamentally different from the one found in *Detective*. Instead of limiting the amount of time spent on a case on the game board, the time mechanic in *Chronicles* serves to add a cost to individual actions across the case, tallied up digitally through the companion app, with the final time affecting the score awarded to the players for successful completion of the case. Also, like *Detective*, *Chronicles* affords the ability for players to refer to older information; however, the game relegated this task to the companion app, allowing players to quickly traverse past screens rather than digging through cards.

The key point where *Chronicles* takes advantage of hybrid mechanics, though, is in players' ability to visually and physically examine a crime scene through a combination of AR/VR and analog cards. To observe a crime scene, one player must use the app (with or without the separately sold VR/3D goggles) to observe the scene and describe what they see to the other players, who pick relevant/matching evidence categories out of the scattered card pile on the table. Players then scan those cards to figure out which evidence is and isn't relevant to the case; however, each scan adds 5 minutes to the case time, forcing players to decide which evidence seems relevant before choosing which to scan. Players can also call in specialists to uncover more information about certain cards, which can lead to more evidence, which in turn can be investigated by other specialists *ad nauseam* – the only limitation being the amount of time players are willing to expend. Additionally, as players visit locations and scan evidence, the narrative evolves within the digital system in such a way that players may want to visit certain individuals to interview them multiple times over the course of the case. As new evidence is uncovered and the story evolves with time, people of interest may be willing to divulge more information, or even change their story, making the players' thorough detective work absolutely critical.

DISCUSSION

The virtual aspects of these hybrid games alter levels of abstraction between player and character, by which I mean they change the metaphorical distance between the two. By scrapping abstracted analog mechanical elements in favor of affording literal analogues to the players' narrative actions, virtual aspects can break down the distinction between player and character. Not completely, of course. You don't forget that you're yourself when playing them, but some of these virtual mechanics – the VR crime scene investigation in *Chronicles*, for example – allow you to engage with the game's narrative in ways that the detective your character represents would. Alternatively, they increase that distinction when they automate non-player-centric system mechanics so that the overall system-focused parts of the game become abstracted to the point that they are no longer the players' concern. *Chronicles*' card-scanning system removes the busywork completely from the investigation, and *Mansions*' app-based monster management means that players can focus on how they react to those monstrous threats, rather than on executing the monsters' mechanics.

But when looking at what these hybrid mechanics actually *do*, an important question comes to mind: what exactly makes for a successful hybrid game design? We can approach this question from a few different angles, but for now we will focus on the design-system-focused and storytelling-focused sides. From a design standpoint, the hybridization is successful when the digital elements integrate and exchange information with the analog elements of the game in such a way that it enables, rather than obstructs, the flow of play. From this perspective, the digital elements should either: (a) make the players do less busywork (like the ANTARES search engine); (b) remove non-player-centric systems from the sphere of player concern (like the "virtual gamemaster" of *Mansions*); or (c) afford player actions that would not be available to them in a purely analog system (e.g., *Chronicle's* VR crime scene investigation). Similarly, I would consider a hybrid design to be successful when they afford player access to additional information that would either be impossible or difficult to achieve in a purely analog system. In this case, "information" can mean anything from words on a page (like the ANTARES database) to affordances that provide abstract thematic information (music and sound design in *Mansions*) or unabstracted visual information (once again, VR crime scenes in *Chronicles*). Hybrid design might also be considered successful when it provides players with additional ways to interact with the world of the game from the positions of their characters through the interfacing of the game's digital and analog elements.

With these elements in place to facilitate storytelling, though, a new, possibly more interesting question arises: how critical are these hybrid elements to storytelling in their games? Are they core systems that allow storytelling to occur? Or are they superfluous pieces of design, not actually necessary for the games to function? In short, the answer depends on the game. For *Detective*, the game's hybrid elements are essential for preserving the thematic focus of the narrative, even if they are not crucial to the narrative itself. The inclusion of digital elements keeps players from getting tied up in papers and parsing, and allows them to focus on the analytical aspects of the game's design. Non-digital *Detective* would play much like *Sherlock Holmes* – still functional, but a fundamentally different experience. The ANTARES database also serves as an organic and diegetic part of the game world for players to interact with and immerse themselves within the same narrative frame as the game's plot. *Mansions'* digital elements, by comparison, are not essential to the game's function, as proven by the existence of the fully analog *Mansions of Madness, 1st Edition*. The digital elements added by the 2nd edition, however, are a clear improvement over their analog counterparts, as they (the digital elements) ease player cognitive load while still enabling additional functions during play.

Lastly, the digital elements of *Chronicles* are fully essential to the game's core experience. Without the ability to examine crime scenes in VR and without the game's ability to adjust the available information and narrative in response to player progress, *Chronicles* simply would not be the same narrative experience. The loss of the self-altering narrative and virtual crime scene environments – along with the card-scanning mechanic around which most of the game is based – would essentially reduce it to a clone of *Sherlock Holmes*. A lack of hybrid storytelling elements would increase players' overall cognitive load, as they are now forced to contend with massive amounts of written case information and must discard the game's most interesting and unique method for delivering its narrative information in the form of the VR crime scene.

Overall, I would argue that while the digital elements of hybrid games are not fully essential to the games' ability to tell a story in general, they *are* essential for creating the specifically tailored narrative experience provided by each game. These hybrid elements can offer an overall better experience by creating story-heavy games that are easier for players to engage with by easing their acquisition of information and reducing the number of complex systems they need to keep track of in order to play the game. These elements also allow for the introduction of interesting alternative mechanics (like *Detective's* evidence matching and the VR crime scene I've already talked so much about) that provide engaging alternatives to forcing players to sift through mountains of text in search of a story.

With the increased complexity that the addition of digital elements adds to the creation of hybrid games, the skills necessary to engage in hybrid game design become more complex as a result. Designers need to understand different ways to structure a story, whether it's crafting a linear narrative for players to experience and then move on, or something more open-ended that allows players to experience the story again with potentially different results. Either way, they have to be able to construct a narrative that can perpetuate player interaction while engaging players on both interactive and thematic levels. They need a solid understanding of how different systems in games (both analog and digital) would interact with one another, and how those systems interface with, build upon, and *are* built upon by the game's narrative. When designers work alone, skills with art (both physical and digital) can help them, even if such skills are not necessarily required. However, knowledge of some level of computer programming is an absolute must. What is required can be as complex as creating VR environments like in *Chronicles* or as simple as customizing a wiki for the game.

Crucially, the designer needs a strong understanding of *why* their game is a hybrid. In the case of *Mansions*, the hybrid elements serve to make play easier on the players. In *Chronicles*, they exist to provide unique ways to interact with the world of the game and further sink players into the shoes of their character. Does the designer's game fit in either of those molds? What about the experience they are trying to create lends itself to the digital aspects they have in mind? Are the hybrid mechanics a part of the game system or the game world? (The ANTARES database is a tool for player characters as much as it is for players, but the digital tools in *Chronicle* are primarily for the benefit of the players with no in-story counterpart.) Does the inclusion of digital elements take away from the experience of the analog, or vice-versa? Designers should, at least, have some idea of the answers to these questions early in the design process in order to help guide creative decisions.

CONCLUSION

Hybrid games, as they move forward, offer a promising avenue for story-telling. Following the path originally laid out by digital story games and the Legacy[1] movement in the analog sphere, designers can find unique and remarkable syntheses of storytelling elements from both media to create novel and unique experiences that would otherwise be impossible. While these experiences are not fully essential to the general storytelling ability of analog games (there have been many games in the analog sphere already and many in the aforementioned Legacy movement that tell, or at least try to tell, stories), the digital elements introduced into hybrid games contribute to the essential narrative experiences of these games. These hybrid designs innovate on past experiences to provide players with immersive ana-logs to in-fiction actions. They also facilitate evolving narrative worlds while minimizing the cognitive load shouldered by the players. Accordingly, these hybrid designs have the potential to push past the perceived limitations on both analog and digital games storytelling in years to come.

---

[1] That is, an analog game whose basic design allows for it to change over time through playable ses-sions, like roleplaying game ("RPG") campaigns. For a deeper discussion, please review Maurice Suckling's chapter in this book. – R.B.

CHAPTER 7

The Shape of Story

Matt Parker

CONTENTS

THERE'S A JOB FOR THAT?

Wait, so help me understand, you're an engineer? No. *An architect?* Well... uh, no. *A contractor?* Not really, no.

This is how the conversation always begins. Followed promptly by the appropriately confounding question, *Then who's building the rides and designing the parks?*

It's a fair question. Who does design theme parks? There's so much that goes into them: Fantastical lands, enchanting attractions, nighttime spectaculars, walk-around characters, delectable dining, and oh, lest we forget the material treatment of an attraction's ceiling, the sound design of a gift shop, or the layout of guest pathways. And that's just the front-of-house!

We haven't even touched on back-of-house (off-stage) design and operations for the army of employees who actually has to work there day in and day out. All of which brings us back to that one lingering question, *Who does design theme parks?* The answer: Many people, from many disciplines, with many different ideas, all banding together, to create lightning in a bottle. Welcome to the wonderful world of themed entertainment design.

My name is Matt Parker, and I am a creative director for attractions, shows, live events, and resort destinations. I have had the unique pleasure of creating, designing, installing, and opening a variety of shows and attractions for beloved franchises such as *Looney Tunes*, DC Comics, *Harry Potter*, *The Hunger Games*, and the *Twilight* saga. From ground-breaking VR simulator attractions to nighttime, mapped-projection spectaculars, to charming family entertainment centers, the beauty of themed entertainment design is that no project is ever the same. In this chapter, we will take a closer look at the process of attraction design, story development basics in an attraction experience, challenges and responsibilities for designers to consider, and ways to break into the industry.

Ready? All right then. Please remain seated, keep your hands and arms inside the vehicle, and refrain from flash photography. Your journey is about to begin.

THE DESIGN PROCESS

The process of themed entertainment design follows a similar evolution to that of architecture and construction, broken down into eight phases: strategy and vision, concept design, schematic design, design development, construction drawings, manufacturing and production, integration and programming, training and show quality control.

Below is a brief breakdown of what each phase entails:

1. **Strategy and Vision**: During this initial phase, the design team may audit the site, review project parameters, and discuss client goals, followed by an assessment of fitting opportunities and an overall vision.

2. **Concept Design**: Dream BIG! Understand the project parameters but push the boundaries. This is the "yes and" phase, inviting the most high-flying ideas into the conversation, and defining the overarching story concept and design.

3. **Schematic Design**: How much will this *really* cost? This phase begins to put real numbers to ideas, as both designers and producers work

together to qualify what is the best way to mitigate ballooning expenses, while maintaining creative goals.

4. **Design Development**: In preparation for construction drawings, this phase completes the details of the design effort, attaching real-world numbers to the designs, making it possible to pull ideas off the page and into reality.

5. **Construction and Shop Drawings**: Produced either in-house or in partnership with other vendors, the construction drawings define the physical architecture, show sets, props, costumes, and anything a guest will see, hear, or otherwise experience.

6. **Manufacturing and Production**: Based off the aforementioned drawings or other forms of documentations (such as show scripts, character models, etc.), these show elements are now produced for use in the park.

7. **Integration and Programming**: On-site installation teams take ownership of the physical spaces and install everything from show sets and media content to lighting and special effects. After, or oftentimes during installation, show programmers dial in the show cues and timing.

8. **Training and Show Quality Control**: Before handover to park operations, the onsite installation teams train park operations and stress test the attraction(s) to ensure repeated peak performance over a period of ride or show cycles.

Throughout one's career in themed entertainment, myriad projects and clients will require a deeper understanding of each phase in order to better accomplish the project goals. If some of these terms sound unfamiliar, do not fret or fear; the design process is a baseline for all stakeholders to better understand the timeline and goals. Speaking of stakeholders, let's discuss the different types of vested parties and how their goals will influence your story and design.

WORKING WITH STAKEHOLDERS

In addition to understanding the design process, it's also important to understand stakeholder involvement and goals. Typically, theme park designers are contracted by one of three types of clients: an existing operator, an intellectual property owner, or a developer. But how do they differ? Well, it's typically quite simple. A developer will primarily focus their efforts on how best to maximize the value of their site (physical, not digital). An existing operator evaluates current and future metrics, seeking new ways to increase incremental attendance and revenue. Lastly, an IP owner is charged with representing their brand in the best possible way to increase brand engagement and reach. With these factors in mind, let's take a closer look at some examples below to better understand how stakeholders may influence and inform a story's development during different phases of design.

At the onset of design, we begin with an audit and establish a strategy and vision for the experience. Consider a developer's opening schedule and site impact. In this scenario, a developer might have a target opening date of 3 years; however, the site (thanks to site studies and feasibility reports) might require a hefty amount of terraforming to meet the goals of the designer's initial vision for story design and park layout. In this scenario, designers may have to rethink their vision for the park's story and design, and instead lean into the existing site layout in order to open within the required timeline.

In another scenario, a park operations team might request concepts for a new attraction. However, one note from the operations team is that they need this attraction to have a high-throughput THRC. THRC stands for *Theoretical Hourly Ride Capacity*, and is a fancy way of defining the maximum number of people who can experience a given attraction within an hour. Understanding that goal, we immediately know that guest agency via virtual reality is out of the question because the time to load and unload guests will not meet the throughput goals for the park operations teams.

Finally, consider the goals of an IP owner during the story development and design. Oftentimes, if a property has been around long enough, the author and audiences have seen the characters, stories, and worlds of the source material change over time. For example, DC Comics has seen myriad iterations of their characters and requisite stories throughout the years. Some for the page, others for the screen, and designers do not always have *carte blanche* to pick and pull from the canon. Consequently, designers often discover an iterative give-and-take with the authors to handpick the best characters and stories to fit within the parks. There are a multitude of reasons why an author may request specific storylines and characters, from future media tie-ins to rearview nostalgia to site-specific localization.

For you, the storyteller, always consider the project goals and stakeholder vision before diving too deep down the rabbit hole. Tap into the wellspring of shared knowledge and resources to ensure a consistent vision that delivers on time and budget, exceeding investor and guest expectations. You have the power to be the attraction's North Star. Shepherd that vision and watch in wonder as one moment's spark of inspiration materializes into a thrilling new experience.

STORY DEVELOPMENT

The journey from idea to opening begins with the same question: "What if?" For example, what if guests could experience the feeling of flight, take agency of their favorite characters, or experience a new story each time they ride? Questions like these kick-start the creative, encouraging teams from a wide breadth of disciplines to consider novel approaches to the guest experience. These blue sky questions empower designers to circle around a big idea, and now, with the seed of that idea, it is time to define the story.

Across the wide-ranging types of show and attractions, there are typically three types of ways in which stories are expressed: plot-driven, plot recitation, or celebrational. The plot-driven story is typically based on existing source material and creates lateral content in the same universe or even time frame but is not a beat-for-beat recitation of the source material. It is not uncommon for a plot-driven story to follow the structure of Joseph Campbell's theory on the *Hero's Journey*. Aboard this attraction, guests will hear the call to action, meet the mentor, test their wits, face off with a deadly foe, seize the reward, and return safely home, venerated as a hero.

Take, for example, a contemporary attraction that has seen clones around the world, *Transformers: The Ride* at Universal Studios theme parks. *Transformers: The Ride* is what is referred to as an indoor, motion-based dark ride. Simply put, a dark ride is any attraction that is partially or wholly inside of a show building that is host to a multitude of scenes containing animated figures, media, theatrical lighting, and special effects. It carries the claim "motion-based" due to the design and movement of the ride vehicle, allowing for six degrees of freedom. This allows the ride programmers to treat the vehicle like a cabin simulator that can pitch, roll, heave, yaw, sway, and surge in synchronization with media and/or with practical effects along a guided track.

When guests step foot inside the queue, they have one mission: Secure the Allspark (this attraction's McGuffin, or plot-driven goal) and get to safety. Sounds easy enough. But then come the attacks. A series of melees, bouts, and escape maneuvers pits guests against some of the film's most iconic enemies. When all is lost, and it looks like guests are defeated, they (and their mentor) make one last stand, choosing fight over flight.

Rising to the challenge, guests defeat the all-feared Decepticon head honcho, *Megatron*, and return as the victor with the Allspark in hand. It's important to note that, in this attraction, while the unseen driver is making an active choice to engage in the fight, guests do not take a *physical* active role in that participation. This constitutes what can be characterized as a more passive, "lean back" experience versus more recent attractions like *Smuggler's Run* at Disney's *Galaxy's Edge* wherein guests actively take the reins, and their interactive prowess has an immediate impact on the outcome of the story structure. This decision – whether to engage guests in the story with physical interactive input or purely with emotional investment – is a choice for designers to consider when developing a story in the early phases of design. I would argue that both devices are effective ways in which to tell a story, but its success can only be measured in its design execution, which begs the most important question: Does the technology help tell a better story? Or, does technology become the story?

Considering these questions, let's take a closer look at why *Transformers: The Ride* is so successful. First and foremost, this attraction delivers in spades on guest expectations. Whether guests have a cursory or comprehensive knowledge of the canon, the characters, environments, effects, camera moves, and audio all deliver on brand expectations. Second, while the ride does not possess tactile, interactive technology, it is sheer technological feat that comprises a motion-based ride vehicle coupled with IMAX-sized, action-packed scene sequences (plus incredible theatrical and special effects). The experience is a jaw-dropper from beginning to end. Lastly, it touches on the emotional hallmarks of the classic Hero's Journey. From trepidation to triumph, this attraction creates a hero with every ride cycle.

Separate from the plot-driven story is the plot recitation story, or what is commonly referred to as the "book report" version of the attraction's original source material. This story conceit delivers a condensed version of a known property. Many of the dark rides found in Disneyland's *Fantasyland* are abridged versions of their cinematic source material. While these might be book reports, and that might conjure up misgivings about these attractions, there's a reason why these attractions continue to enchant guests of all ages: perspective. Oftentimes, traditional dark rides position guests as the camera in an experience. That is, a camera that moves around and through the story as a third party, watching the major plot points unfold in linear show scenes, much like watching a CliffsNotes version of your favorite film. But clever designers have broken down the proverbial fourth wall. For example, at Disneyland's *Snow White's Enchanted Wish*, guests do not *just* watch Snow White confront the Wicked Witch; guests embody Snow White and come face-to-face with the Wicked Witch. For a young child to figuratively step into the shoes of Snow White and see the Wicked Witch make eye contact with them is a powerful device that goes beyond the book report and reimagines an exciting new way in which guests can experience a familiar story.

Lastly, the celebrational story isn't as much a linear story structure as it is a celebration of themes and environments. Take, for example, Disney's much adored and timeless boat ride, *It's a Small World*. In this attraction, there is no call to action, there is no hero to champion, no villain to defeat, or trials to be had. This story does not use plot to move guests from one scene to the next. Its simplicity is its greatness. It's a celebration of children, culture, and a shared sense of humanity and compassion.

Whether an attraction experience utilizes the plot-driven, plot recitation, or celebration method is a decision that designers and clients will determine to best share their characters and worlds with their guests. Once determined, it is now up to the team to develop ways in which a story is delivered. Let's take a closer look and decode one of themed entertainment's most beloved and time-tested attractions, Disneyland's *The Haunted Mansion*.

THE ATTRACTION EXPERIENCE

The Approach

When we consider any attraction, we must always consider the emotional journey of a guest. Before a guest sets foot inside a queue, boards a vehicle, or ventures off into the unknown, there is that magical moment of discovery. That moment when one rounds a bend, presses through a narrow artery, or peers up in awe at what stands before them. The approach is your opportunity to hint at, tease, or change the tone of a guest's physical surroundings and physiological feedback. It's a moment of pure awe and wonder. The approach is a designer's most valuable preamble to the story. It's the moment of anticipation.

The Disney parks first installation of *The Haunted Mansion* made its park debut in Anaheim, California at Disneyland Park on August 12, 1969. Designed in a manner to draw guests in, there is a reason why the mansion is slightly offset at the far end of the square. It exists on its own, separate from the heart of New Orleans Square, like a lone character, looming in the distance. It piques curiosity and demands investigation. Its very nature, by design, incites anticipation.

With its antebellum-era architecture, towering trees, and its stark off-white treatment, the mansion stands out amidst the tableau and draws guests near with subtle changes. Thanks to nuanced shifts in landscaping, architecture, and audio, guests not only see variations in the world around them, but more importantly, they feel it. It's the feeling of change, the question of "What comes next?"

The Queue

The queue is a fancy way of describing the ill-dreaded line. For years, the queue was nothing more than a series of switchbacks, dropped into a rectangular plot of land in plain sight of the attraction. It invited boredom and resentment, leaving most parents with impatient children and nothing to capture their imagination. Thankfully, the queue has transformed, and *The Haunted Mansion* is an excellent example of how a queue can create a sense of mystery and intrigue.

Beyond New Orleans Square, guests are drawn past iron gates and into well-tended gardens. Instead of unpleasant switchbacks, this queue meanders through a masterfully crafted garden that swiftly turns sideways with a pet cemetery, off-kilter tombstones, and eerie architecture in sight. Whether a guest breezes past the details or indulges them, a series of visual gags alludes to the tone and tenor of the experience to follow. From a series of pun-laden tombstones such as *Wee G. Bord* and *Metta Fisiks* to a horse-less carriage that occasionally nickers to a chandelier enveloped in cobwebs, the successful queue captures the imagination, incites the inquiring mind, and engages guests with the clever use of stage theatrics.

The Preshow Experience

I have to admit, the preshow is quite often my favorite part of the attraction experience. Weird, right? One would assume that the preshow is no more than a safety spiel (that is, an announcement of rules and precautions), and while for some attractions that may be true, these days the preshow is, more often than not, the call to action. Sometimes action-packed, other times whimsical, and in the case of *The Haunted Mansion*, the preshow is a deliciously, devilish appetizer for the entree to follow.

Entering the mansion's main foyer, guests step into an octagonal, windowless room, adorned with paintings on each wall. Keeping to the story, guests are asked to move to the *dead center of the room*, a clever play on words that continues the use of *pun fun* as found in the preceding queue. With guests loaded into the preshow, they are welcomed to the beginning of their tour. Moments later, the room appears to stretch, revealing macabre paintings that adorn the walls. A *Ghost Host* (via a recorded character actor) begs the question: *Is this haunted room actually stretching? Or is it one's imagination?* Moments later, the lights flicker, the foyer goes dark, and a corpse hangs from the attic above. A maniacal cackle, then... one chilling solution: *"Of course, there's always my way."*

So, what does this preshow accomplish? To begin with, it establishes that guests have been invited inside this mansion to experience a tour. Second, it sets the tone: dark, macabre. Finally, it poses a challenge, or better still, a call to action for guests to get out... alive! This last beat is a nod to a larger story that unfolds just moments later when guests learn that the mansion is host to 999 souls, with room for one more... *"Any volunteers?"* This clever prompt clearly defines the story parameters, creates active participation for the guest, and most importantly, begs the question for each and every guest: *Will I make it out alive?* Step right up, it's time to find out.

The Ride Experience

This is it! Everything has been leading up to this. The main show.

Be it a simulator, story coaster, flying theater or any number of ride systems, the preceding moments of anticipation, mystery, and intrigue are now, finally, about to pay off. Reverting to our emotional curve, this is the calm before the storm. At vehicle load, it's an opportunity to give guests a false sense of security, or in the case of *The Haunted Mansion*, a moment's reprieve, where flickering candlelight and cobweb-covered chandeliers set the stage for the tour to follow.

Guests are loaded into their ride vehicles and venture off into the first act of the attraction. Around a dark bend, guests are deposited into a hallway of doors, where handles turn, ghosts knock, and corridors never end. It's an eerie entree, but like any good monster movie, it sets up the chills and thrills without even the slightest sighting. This moment builds anticipation; it creates uncertainty, discomfort, and the slightest hint of fear. Rounding a corner, guests discover a seance, or what we may refer to as the story's inciting incident. Amidst this scene, the mystic, Madame Leota, calls upon the spirits to materialize. Thanks to her otherworldly frequencies and the guests' spirited vibrations, a connection is made, and guests are about to be transported to a new world.

In the next scene, guests come face-to-face with a ballroom celebration, only to learn that it's a wake... in their honor! Suddenly the tables have turned – no longer are guests mere mortals watching from afar.

Now they are welcome participants, a part of the story, and, maybe, a fixture in the mansion. The core of the ride attraction takes guests through a series of scenes inside and outside of the mansion where grinning ghosts of all shapes and sizes serenade their slow-moving house guests. By the end of the attraction, guests do, in fact, find their way out. Albeit, there is one surprising caveat as told by our illustrious host. For this kiss goodnight[1], the last scene takes place in a hallway of mirrors, wherein – thanks to a little Disney sorcery – guests delight in a haunted hitchhiker who's come along for the ride home! After a moment of laughter and a breath of relief, guests giggle alongside their friendly, hitchhiking ghouls and rest peacefully knowing that the afterlife is a spirited soiree that patiently awaits their imminent return.

The Post-Show and Gift Shop

After disembarking, guests board a conveyance that carries them back to the land of the living. However, before leaving, there's one last post-show moment, one final kiss goodnight[2] as guests bid farewell to the immortal. Perched on a ledge, one of the mansion's eldest ghouls encourages guests to: *"Hurry back... Make final arrangements now. We've been dying to have you."* It's a moment of levity, buttoned up nicely with a welcome invitation to return to this happy haunt where there's always room for one more. While the Anaheim version of this attraction does not have an immediate gift shop to follow, the Orlando attraction and other similar versions around the world promptly deposit guests into the gift shop.

There's a reason why most major attractions drop guests into a themed gift shop – relief and reward. Think about it: guests answered a call to action, explored uncharted frontiers, confronted heinous villains, and conquered their fears. For that, they deserve not only a sense of relief, but also a reward, often in the form of a totem, charm, or plush doll that declares, *I did it!* It is a takeaway keepsake that reminds guests of that spectrum of emotions usually reserved for feature films, Broadway musicals, or book series, and now serves as an extension of the brand, engaging guests from afar.

From the moment a guest first sets eyes on the approach or purchases a keepsake in the gift shop, the guest journey continues to evolve, immersing

---

[1] Disney-speak for that final, unforgettable moment that ends the experience on a high note. Not to be confused with the 2-minute feel-good farewell that signals the closing of the Magic Kingdom every night. – R.B.

[2] Ibid.

them both physically and emotionally into the story. As audiences continue to expect the unexpected, designers of tomorrow are tasked with creating new ways to engage guests and create thrilling new attractions. Now that we understand the pillars of today's successful attractions, let's look into Madame Leota's crystal ball and conjure up apparitions of the future.

THE FUTURE OF THEMED ENTERTAINMENT

Agency and Immersion

With a deeper understanding of the attraction experience, it's time to ask ourselves, *What is the future of themed entertainment?*

Agency.

Which is also the future of themed entertainment design. It's the opportunity for guests to not only engage with their favorite characters, but also become them. It's the ability for them to forge new paths and explore uncharted lands. It's the realization that every guest can experience their own journey, can be the hero of their own story, and can create a relationship to the story and its characters in uniquely memorable ways. Think back to the first time E.T. bid you farewell at Universal's *E.T. Adventure*, or when you cast your first spell at *Diagon Alley*, or piloted the Millennium Falcon at Disney's *Galaxy's Edge*. These stories are personalized extensions of their source material, where every guest can walk in the footsteps of their favorite Jedi, Wizard, or Superhero. But beware, agency does not equate to a video game. Agency is more than taking control of a joystick, mashing buttons, or matching interactive gestures. Agency is both a physical and emotional connection to the experience, providing guests with the opportunity to interact with worlds, characters, and stories like never before.

How does one do this? Emotional immersion.

I'll admit it, I love to throw around the word "immersion." In fact, I'd go so far as to say that most artists pander to the newfound idea of immersing a guest in their experience, be it a film, television show, art installation, or theme park attraction. Sure, immersion is important. No, it's more than important – it's necessary. A guest, viewer, or patron needs to feel completely consumed, swallowed whole by the artist's intent, untethered to their reality, and transported to new worlds. But it *must* be more than just a pretty facade. After all, if you can't hear the voices in the walls, then your place-making has lost its most important feature – character. In themed entertainment design, to understand story is to understand design. They are not two separate entities; rather, they coexist every step of the way.

To be frank, the term "emotional immersion" is not a commonly used term. It is, in my eyes, an augmentation of the obvious. Immersion is a necessity, but I would encourage you to think bigger than just pretty facades or time-traveling lands, and to understand that design must be informed by the emotional beat of the experience. But what exactly does that mean? Let's, for a moment, consider film and television. When we think about a traditional feature-length film or television show, there is a process called *color grading*. This is a process by which the director and the director of photography will work with a colorist to help *augment* the mood of the scene by way of color. If a scene is more somber and wistful, it might have cooler shades of blue. If a scene is upbeat and warm, it may utilize warmer shades of amber and gold. If a scene is foreign, toxic, or discomforting, it may utilize shades of green and purple. This filmmaking technique helps filmmakers immerse viewers deeper into the emotional context of the scene.

In themed entertainment, color is used in similar ways to evoke feelings and emotional shifts. But also, we can *color* an environment with different techniques, for example, with sound. When we created a land inspired by the *Twilight* saga films at Lionsgate Entertainment World in Zhuhai, China, we knew that we wanted to immerse guests into the protagonist Bella's hometown of Forks, Washington. However, due to architectural constraints, we could only create facades, and unfortunately could not invite guests into the charming storefronts that pepper the small, forested town. What materialized were some lovely facades and theatrical twilight lighting. However, the land lacked character, it lacked life, and it lacked presence. Working with a team of talented sound designers, we developed a series of soundscapes for both the town and the surrounding forest. Today, when guests step foot into Forks, they are enveloped in the inviting, diegetic sounds of a small town in the Pacific Northwest, replete with passing motors, bike bells, distant horns, and a comforting bed of warbling birds and trilling insects. These sounds are warm, welcoming, and inviting. By contrast, as guests venture out into the forest, en route for the attractions, those city sounds dissipate and give way to the bucolic sounds of natural wildlife, rustling leaves, and gentle breezes. These sounds are a warning; they are anticipatory, steeped in mystery and trepidation. By way of using sound as color, we created not only a sense of physical and transportive immersion but also an emotional connection to the physical environment that pulls guests deeper into the story.

PARTING THOUGHTS
Your Big Break

No matter how much information one can impart, there always remains the question: *How do I get my big break?* Today, there are opportunities aplenty to find your way into the business.

On the collegiate level, there are now, more than ever before, a multitude of junior colleges and universities that offers academic tracks created specifically for the themed entertainment business. In addition, as we've established by now, themed entertainment is not a singular track, and academic institutions are broadening their reach into game design, transmedia, and emerging technologies. If there's a specific department of themed entertainment that interests you more than others, pursue it no matter the department it's in! Enjoy writing? Consider a degree in Creative Writing. Enjoy ride systems design? Consider mechanical engineering. Have a passion for conceptual design? Think about studying art history, and imagine the breadth of knowledge you will develop. Bottom line: the more equipped you are when you come to the table, the more valuable you are in this field.

To share a brief personal story, when I was 12, I started to pursue a passion for themed entertainment. I met a retired theme park Imagineer who mentored me and taught me the broad strokes of how to write and design the guest experience. At the time, media integration was relatively new, and he suggested exploring media production as a backdoor into the business. That suggestion turned into a shared passion for filmmaking and theme park design (a backstory you will encounter with many in the business). As I got older and attended college, I studied filmmaking and creative writing. Several years later, I stumbled upon a video on Imagineering, and learned that there were, in fact, jobs in the business for a writer – or, as it's known in the industry, "show writer." Now, as someone who didn't have a strong artistic wrist, was not terribly good at math, and had little interest in management, I had, before then, given up. However, upon discovering this bit of news, I immediately set out to reach out to every show writer I could find. Jumping into the TEA guide (TEA stands for Themed Entertainment Association), I cold-called a handful of writers and creative directors. While the response rate was limited, two fantastically talented show writers did respond – one of whom became another incredible mentor who helped me better understand the craft, and the other became a wonderful friend and colleague.

This business is a small one. Go out there and meet people. Share experiences together. Find similarities. Go to parks and attractions together. Discuss what you enjoyed, and what you might've done differently. Want to really understand how a park works? Go work at one. Hundreds of incredible designers have, at some point in their lives, worked a summer or several years in the parks. Soak up the world of themed entertainment. Watch how guests interact with design, cast members, and each other. Like any creative job, there is no straight line; it's a series of instincts and iterations.

I will leave you with these final thoughts: Never stop learning, revel in the details, and above all, find your voice. Take the time to explore it, shape it, and when you're ready, share it.

Red Flags

Ross Berger

CONTENTS

WRITERS OF BOOKS, TV, film, and other media face myriad challenges once they hit a single key on the keyboard or press their pen against a pad. These challenges are mostly creative in nature – fixing a plot point, polishing a sentence, what have you. It's no easy task, the race toward perfection; a finish line is truly never crossed. But fiction writers in high technology cannot focus on their craft alone. New technologies, by nature of the beast, are in constant flux. Frequent innovation forces an identity crisis of the technology that, thereby, forces writers to accommodate challenges outside of their craft daily, if not hourly. Upholding the craft becomes secondary to serving the needs of the technology.

While best practices are the focus of this book, I must admit that it can be hard to maintain them in a professional environment when technology

DOI: 10.1201/9781003141594-9

changes so often. There are always surprises within a single challenge. This happens in any work environment, no matter the industry or expertise of the employee. But there are different rules for high technology, and I'd be remiss if I didn't discuss common red flags or indicators of concern that persist, year after year, no matter the company, that not only affect one's job as a storyteller but also affect the consumer. Not all companies will succumb to common red flags, and a single company may not necessarily succumb to all common red flags; yet, red flags pop up frequently and suddenly, so it's best to prepare for them.

A company's feverish rush to enter the market with an innovation can come at great cost. Employees are often powerless to the shortcomings of the final product. This is expected. But there are ways within your power to assure that the ship (or at least your side of it) does not hit the iceberg up ahead. And there are always icebergs, even if they vary in size. Start-ups or established companies looking to launch a new product category often face the biggest of icebergs, for a single wrong move can sink the company or department overnight.

As a storyteller, you are required to be flexible; that will be your greatest skill. As new technologies emerge, their rulesets for telling a good story will expand and contract, stabilize and fluctuate, until an audience of profitability sets in, upon which time companies rest on their laurels and innovate in only the smallest and safest ways. Until that day, one must protect their craft while navigating the tides of flux in the entertainment and technology worlds.

RED FLAG #1: ONE SIZE FITS ALL (NOT REALLY)

In traditional media like film or television, genre dictates the types of stories an audience will experience. Film noir, for instance, seldom has a happy ending. There are archetypes (femme fatale), specific conflicts (heist gone wrong, the double cross), and cinematic techniques (dark photography) that convey the genre's essence. Audiences, therefore, have certain expectations when they watch a film noir. The same goes for comedy, horror, drama, etc.

Similarly, though not obviously, the medium through which a story is told also possesses similar rules and expectations. Digital content and television are episodic experiences where a longstanding narrative is told over time. Books and film, in a one-shot deal (sequels not counted). But when new storytelling platforms emerge, tech and media companies often ignore or minimize the consumption patterns of the audience or user.

These consumption patterns include: through which technology does a consumer, say, watch a movie; how much does he/she watch at a given time; does he/she yield just partial concentration because they are multitasking? For example, someone watching *The Dark Knight Returns* on their phone is likely to disrupt their viewing experience frequently, watch it in chunks, or maybe never finish it. Why? Because the showcase through which they are watching it (aka the phone) is designed for on-the-go activities, where numerous small tasks can be accomplished quickly in between more meaningful events like work meetings, dental appointments, or class. Therefore, native content for the phone conforms to disruptive, quick-burst consumption patterns typically found in mobile games and digital episodic content.

Yet, companies do not always understand this. They commonly think that because millions of people saw *The Dark Knight Returns* in the movie theater and a smaller yet impressive number downloaded it on iTunes or Google Play that a repurposed version (or a copycat story with different but similar worlds and characters) must be created for their new platform or technology. So, they impetuously adopt a universal list of untested ingredients – including but not exclusive to: the medium (2.5-hour film); the visual aesthetic (dark); the genre (superhero) – and spend tens to hundreds of millions of dollars to recreate the magic of the past for technology of the future. And they do so without understanding the bounds of their new technology, without establishing its content grammar and ruleset. The famous adage that "Content is king" is false wisdom. In actuality, platform[1] and content share the same kingdom. How[2] you watch is just as important as what you watch, and with the advent of otherworldly technologies like virtual reality and physical artificial intelligence (e.g., robots or virtual assistants like Alexa and Siri), platform (today) tends to be more compelling than the content on it. We're in the novelty phase of these technologies. Once they grow up and the consumers grow up with them, the content will have to as well.

---

[1] "Platform" is a general term for hardware (e.g., virtual reality headset, video game console, television), software (e.g., online chatbot or A.I., streaming service, web content), or analog medium (e.g., book, magazine, theater, board game; in other words, something that doesn't require electricity or Wi-Fi to experience). Please see this book's introduction under the "Terminology" section.

[2] "How" meaning through which hardware (mobile phone vs. television) or software (live programming, streaming service, or digital download). These examples refer to "lean back" or passive entertainment, like television or film. The "lean forward' or participatory/proactive experiences (like video games or interactive television) have similar hardware and software constraints, though they affect the level of interactivity as well as the viewing experience.

Yet, executives who think "One Size Fits All" fall into an understandable trap. A beloved hit can create enormous profits in side media and merchandising. *Avengers, Transformers, Star Wars* all reap stout profits from toys, comics, and animated shows that bear their names. As we know, it's not repurposed content but expansions of the worlds of the films. Copycat intellectual property also stands to gain a profit too, though not as hefty as those they are copying... unless, of course, the IP was rushed for release sooner than the competition for fear that their product was inferior. Perhaps these "rushed" IPs lacked the star power and/or brand recognition of their rivals. Consider: *Deep Impact* (released: May 8, 1998; earned: $349.5 million worldwide)[3] vs. *Armageddon* (released: July 1, 1998; earned: $553.7 million worldwide)[4]; *Antz* (released: October 2, 1998; earned: $171.8 million worldwide)[5] vs. *A Bug's Life* (released: November 20, 1998; earned: $363.3 million worldwide)[6]; *Dante's Inferno* (released: February 4, 2010; units sold on PS3 + Xbox360: 2 million)[7][8] vs. *God of War III* (released: March 16 2010; units sold on PS3: 7.6 million).[9] Either way, these IPs made considerable money, capitalizing on a recipe that was bound for success no matter what.

Sympathy for the devil – I mean, the executive – extends to the challenge to which they are scaling their content. An unproven platform or technology needs a guinea pig (read: content) to prove itself. If the content isn't recognizable, either through its brand or its genre, it will struggle to attract consumers. Also – and this is a dirty industry secret – if the content is familiar and beloved, executives believe that consumers will forgive the flaws of their new platform – that is: *It's okay if the headset is heavy and disorienting as long as it's cool to see Batman in virtual reality.* This kind of thinking makes sense, in that, you're testing an experimental technology with a safe, successful IP. But seldom are the kinks worked out before launch, and seldom is the marriage between platform and content understood the first, second, or third go-around. Companies know this, yet the conventional wisdom is often ignored.

---

[3] https://www.boxofficemojo.com/title/tt0120647/?ref_=bo_se_r_1
[4] https://www.boxofficemojo.com/title/tt0120591/?ref_=bo_se_r_1
[5] https://www.boxofficemojo.com/title/tt0120587/?ref_=bo_se_r_1
[6] https://www.boxofficemojo.com/title/tt0120623/?ref_=bo_se_r_1
[7] https://www.vgchartz.com/game/32227/dantes-inferno/
[8] https://www.vgchartz.com/games/game.php?id=32240
[9] https://www.vgchartz.com/game/12533/god-of-war-iii/. *God of War* franchise is Sony-exclusive; therefore, there are no sales on non-Sony platforms.

So, you might wonder: When there's so much at stake – i.e., money, reputation, employee morale (yes, in that order) – why does this happen all the time? Why is it nearly impossible to use the ruleset of an established medium and apply it seamlessly to a new platform? Why is it that those in charge fail at repurposing a beloved brand for a new experience?

There are a series of steps that is overlooked for expedience and cost. And, most importantly, no executive wants to look bad if their huge gamble isn't paying off early on; thus, some processes are ignored or de-prioritized. What the "One Size Fits All" model does is endanger the future of the project. Jobs are at stake if the project fails. Yet, one will find a stronger path toward success by identifying: focus testing data regarding consumption patterns; consumer fatigue; and marketplace competition. There's often a big budget to try something new, something daring, and executives shoot for the stars without any regard to the confines just mentioned. Nor is there anyone to rein in the C-Suite because either the groupthink is too pervasive or people are too afraid to say no to the big voices in the room.

But executives also ignore one of the most fundamental elements of the marriage between content and platform, to their detriment, always.

Cognitive Load

There is no science in determining what makes a successful and original experience for VR, an amusement park ride, or a virtual assistant; there are only proximities to success, targeted to the components (e.g., protagonist, villain, visual spectacle) rather than the whole experience. But not all media are translatable to other media. For instance, a good VR story will not always (or ever) make a good virtual assistant story experience, mainly because the physical and cognitive requirements are vastly different from one another. Cognitive load is the main factor here, and it requires one's understanding of the stimuli they are exposed to, the amount of stimuli, the speed by which they can absorb the stimuli, and the capacity to hold all of that stimuli in one thinking moment. Watching a 30-second television commercial that promotes a new CD collection of Motown's greatest musicians is easier to absorb cognitively than a virtual assistant that promotes the same product but communicates its essential information through a monotone voice in the same amount of time *sans* visual accompaniment. The TV commercial has clips of the Four Tops, The Supremes, and Stevie Wonder, giving the viewer a visual and audio reminder of the greatness of that music. The lower third of the screen displays text that reinforces the narration, which communicates the price of the product and the number to call in. Yet, without these visual reminders and the periodic breaks of the narration, the information of the price and the number to call in will either be forgotten or ignored. Our brains can absorb more from a hybrid medium, such as television, where audio and visual work together to communicate not only information but a feel, an emotional connection. Google Assistant and Alexa are disadvantaged in that regard as their primary communication tool is their voice only, and our brains cannot absorb too much of that voice (or any voice) in one sitting. A chime that indicates the end of a request (or that reinforces a brief information "packet") allows our brains to relax and solidify what was just communicated. Under such constraints, Google Assistant and Alexa therefore would collapse as a storytelling device if the "One Size Fits All" model had its way.

Cognitive loads are not immutable, but not significantly so. And yes, there are exceptions. There are people who can absorb more Alexa information at one time than others can. But designers and storytellers are creating for the vast majority of users and their typical engagement with the technology, not for the exceptions to the rule.

In general, with any new medium or technology, customers must often train themselves or rewire their cognitive capacity to absorb and understand the stimuli being sent to them. On the opposite end, developers must learn what the cognitive fatigue limits are for their customers. This takes time to develop. Hearing radio for the first time was vastly different from watching television for the first time or experiencing VR in a headset for the first time. First, there's a shock to the senses, then, gradually, an assimilation to the stimuli. The cognitive limits expand with each use until they plateau. The average users' plateau dictates the ideal length of the content experience in a single use.

Physical Limits of Technology

In the past, however, cognitive load didn't always dictate the length of a content experience. The physical limits of the tech often did. The running time of a film, for instance, conformed to the actual physical length of a roll of film on a single reel. In 1906, the average length was 10 minutes, which rose to 30 minutes by 1910. By the 1920s, that length increased to an hour-and-a-half to 2 hours, the typical range of a film's length today, thanks to innovations that allowed for a seamless hand-off from reel to reel. Obviously, we can no longer attribute today's film length to physical dictates of the film reel; rather, cultural habit is the main factor. The medium has been challenged on many fronts since the 1950s – mainly by television.

But it wasn't until 2006 when film's prominence as the world's preeminent entertainment and cultural medium started to fade significantly.

With the advent of digital media and the rise of YouTube, countless 3–5-minute bite-sized videos sparked the deep interest and addiction of millions of viewers across the world. Why? Because the content on YouTube was short enough to serve as breaks for people already glued to their computers during work or school. In between classes, meetings, or at-home tasks, a consumer could watch, on their laptop, a quick video of new content for *Prom Queen* and *LonelyGirl15*, a music video from Justin Timberlake, or an excerpt of a film or TV show (without license or permission). When the smartphone emerged in 2007, consumers could consume a piece of entertainment while waiting at the doctor's office or at some other destination while on the move – all in the palm of their hand! A movie screen that can fit in their back pocket! The smartphone remains the most successful form factor of any entertainment technology to this day.

Now, the type of content, as opposed to its length, is a bigger nut to crack. A 3-minute one-off video might not carry the same weight for one person as a 3-hour film does for another, even if projected through the same technology. If one is accustomed to using their phone for on-the-go, quick-fix tasks, it's unlikely they'll use it to watch a 3-hour film in one sitting or at all. So, again, one size does not fit all. As the next section will tackle, to determine how a story can be delivered is to establish what the constraints are for that medium and what that medium is primarily used for.

RED FLAG #2: IGNORING CONSUMER EXPECTATIONS

It's a given that not all consumers are the same. Where one might use a butter knife to butter toast, another might use it to open the slot on the back of a remote control to remove its batteries (Not Recommended). Where one might use a text book to learn about a subject for college, another might use it to prop up a laptop on their desk (again, Not Recommended). In other words: every product can be repurposed to service a need outside of its original design. But the customer's intention of that purchase isn't for its repurposed happy accident. (After all, it's not cost-effective to spend $60 on a text book whose sole purpose is to prop, not educate.) This is to say that when a customer buys any product, they expect to leverage its primary expectations. What can it do minimally and what can it do well often occupy the mind of the customer once the product is in use. When the product is stretched outside of its strengths and minimal expectations, a customer is bound for disappointment. But it's not the fault of the customer if they are led to believe the product can do more than it should. In the intersecting world of technology and entertainment, this is the fault of the content creator. Well, more aptly: it is the fault of the C-Suite executives who demand that the content bend to their whims,[10] often incompatibly to the platform or technology. "One Size Fits All" model is not the only culprit; so, too, is the inability to gauge customer expectations properly.

Obviously, setting expectations is much easier when you know what a consumer uses, say, an Alexa device for, or what they expect when they go on an amusement park ride. One might ask: "How much patience do I have for a deep story if I use this platform to check on the status of a package and therefore have a 30-second engagement with it?" Or: "When I am on an amusement park ride, can I absorb information (*ala* plot points or character details) if I am on the verge of dropping 150 feet or traveling 35 mph on a track (or simulations thereof)?" Yet, while these boundaries of expectations are rigid, entrepreneurs ignore them because they believe they have created an unprecedented experience or product that will break all the rules. Yes, a few do. But most don't. Those who do, historically, *stumble* upon a breakthrough, not calculate one.

Throwing everything against the wall and seeing what sticks are necessary. Innovative ways to tell stories are no different. Thus, the red flag here isn't the exploration of what works and what doesn't. Rather, it's the flagrant disregard of what customers expect and want. If a leader thinks he/she can move the needle by forcing customers to reacquaint themselves with a product or technology differently than they had before, failure is around the corner. Look at Quibi, the failed 6-month mobile-only streaming service of original content. Or, the initial laggard sales of the XboxOne when it touted itself as an entertainment hub rather than a gaming device (anemically remedied even after the ouster of a Xbox corporate vice president). The latter example shows that you can't pull the wool over the eyes of die-hard fans, the same people who drive consistent sales, year after year. Telling them that gaming is now secondary to a potential panoply of conventional entertainment and media just to appeal to non-gamers is a strict branding play, and it is one that insults that overwhelming base of customers. The XboxOne does have the technological capacity to play video, to have live (and non-live) interactive experiences of traditional media, but

---

[10] Whims that are data-driven, mind you, but without full context of the emerging marketplace or without scalable focus testing.

that's not what its audience wants either primarily or secondarily. Ignoring their needs stymied the sales of the XboxOne for its entire lifecycle. As for Quibi, the mobile-only experience for unproven content led to an obvious demise. People who are on-the-go with their content and tech welcome the disruption of the entertainment if the intellectual property is something they're already familiar with. Then, they take risks with newer content. If the new platform doesn't offer familiarity either with established IP, beloved actors, or IP that has a near identical feel to something beloved and established, audiences will not follow. So, when it comes to content innovation in the tech space, two general rules emerge: first, good leaders don't force, they incentivize; second, they *don't* know better than the customer. Ever.

RED FLAG #3: FOCUSING ON THE HOLES IN THE ROOF WHEN THE HOUSE IS ON FIRE

The temptation is strong to create something new; it's possibly overwhelming. The bright shiny new object – be it a VR headset, an interactive toy, or a virtual assistant – inspires numerous creative visions within a single team. These visions are relentless, heartfelt and, at times, uncompromising. Yet, they come from a place of genuine love and innovative spirit for the prospective experience. It (the experience) is untested, and thus no one knows what will work, what will not. Those with strong visions will doubt those with equal or greater confidence. In fact, as mentioned above, greatness is stumbled upon, not calculated; therefore, one's vision, no matter how profound, may not be greater or worse than their coworker's. Focus testing provides a direction toward customer likes and dislikes, but it's not a golden path toward success; it's more so a proximity around it; even then, there are no guarantees. Customers are fickle. New products hit the market and can shape expectations differently than what your team has been planning. Your team pivots in response, tech and content change, more focus testing ensues, and just when you think you've hit the right formula, a new product or experience enters the market and disrupts customer tendencies once again.

The chase is frustrating, but it's part of the game. Pivots happen often; in fact, they're encouraged. However, there comes a time when a team must commit toward a single vision of the product and its release date, or they'll be spinning their wheels until the cash dries out and lay-offs saddle a once promising company.

Focus testing is a critical part of the development process. It's somewhat counterintuitive to writing a good story though. Changing plot points and characters based on the whims of random people who are paid nominally to give their opinion on something out of context (or not in its full glory) is immensely frustrating. Yet, focus testing is part of the tech world, and it's not going away any time soon.

As valuable as focus testing is, its data can be easily manipulated and weaponized. People use slices of the data often to validate low hanging fruit/easy wins to inflate the overall positivity of the product or feature. Sometimes, they'll use different slices to show weaknesses in the work of other teams in order to settle interdepartmental rivalries, forcing a reprioritization of budget and employee resources to shape the product toward a jaundiced direction.

The data are only as good as their input. Take, for example, a scenario where you, the writer, need to test the likeability of a new character named Shermy. You didn't write the following survey questions, yet they somehow went through the testing pipeline. The questionnaire comprises the following:

1. Do you think Shermy is handsome with those gigantic, jagged teeth?

2. Do you find it funny when he says lines like: "Yeah, you bet" or "I appreciate that"?

3. What secret do you think he's hiding from his best friend?

The character Shermy doesn't have chance out of the gate. Question #1 undermines itself by cherry picking and emphasizing visual data that is unflattering. Question #2 takes very mundane lines and asks a testing participant to focus just on those lines that do not evoke laughable or interesting memories. Question #3 implies Shermy is deceptive by withholding important information from one of the most important people in his life.

Yes, these are greatly exaggerated questions, but they suffer not only from bias against a character, but also hyper-specificity, taxing the participant to remember minute details that may or may not yield an accurate answer. The data from this test are throw-away.

Over-indexing toward the vague, however, will not achieve better results. Consider the following:

1. Do you like Shermy?

2. Does Shermy make you laugh?

3. Is Shermy a character you want to care for?

While these might seem like fair questions, positive and unchallenging, they do not measure a participant's true desire. It doesn't matter if the character is likeable. There are a ton of likeable characters in fiction. It matters whether or not you want to play Shermy (if you're testing a video game), watch Shermy (if it's a TV show), or buy his branded t-shirt (if it's merchandise). The questions, therefore, need to test a participant's desire for engagement with that character. Explicit questions that call that out – "Do you want to engage Shermy in a video game?" – will fail as well because people are open to ideas of possibilities when asked a general question and will hardly naysay it. But when questions provoke thought and put the participant in the mind of the character, then the truth comes out.

1. How do you think Shermy would respond if a robot spilled soup on his cowboy boots?

2. Of all the activities you've experienced in the last year, which one do you think Shermy would've made a good companion on?

3. In 3 years from now, what kind of adventure would you like see to Shermy on?

If the participant responds with highly detailed answers that take the question seriously, then you are – correctly – measuring for intensity and emotional investment. If the responses are spare, void, or indifferent, the character is not resonating. You need to change course.

While these questions test the components of a story (namely, character), the same approach applies to tech features, art, design, new modules, what have you. Keep in mind if you test just the details (such as feature, module, level, etc.) and not the whole experience, you are solving for minutia and not for significance. In other words, you're missing the point. (The same goes for a story: are you testing the characters in isolation and not how they fit inside the story? Failure paves your way forward.)

Not solving for significance is, as this section's heading reads, the house on fire. Not solving for significance results from many impulses: inability to understand the product's true foundational problems; insecurity with your solutions; and/or a narcissism that leads to the weaponizing or manipulating of focus testing data. The latter is clearly the most destructive of the three, and it can be, sadly, an impulse from leadership.

Thankfully, it doesn't occur frequently, but when it does occur, the red flag is easy to spot from far away. When a product or experience is floundering, everyone notices. "Why is it not meeting expectations?" is met with infinite solutions that are easy and cosmetic, that fix the symptoms and not the disease. "Why is it not meeting expectations" is another way of saying, "Why is it not working?" Is the issue functionality? Is the issue about fun? Is the issue about engagement (as in, are consumers not playing with it enough)? The answer is often clear, but no one wants to recognize it aloud. A floundering product is one whose design and purpose run counter to the preferences of the target demographic. When it is clear that the product is floundering by the majority – if not, by a vocal plurality – of the workforce, it is often too late to change the design and purpose without changing the technology and content wholesale. Years of development are at stake, and no one wants to admit to themselves that the time spent in development was a waste. True: no one knows for sure if the product will fail. But if the solution to fixing an unpopular story of an amusement park ride is changing the colors of the seats, failure is the next stop.

RED FLAG #4: JUST BECAUSE IT CAN DOESN'T MEAN IT SHOULD

The previous red flags apply to any employee or contractor in the tech world. But there's one red flag that stands out especially for writers when product development isn't running according to plan. A common mistake by technology companies is to hire a writer to create a story experience to cover up, distract from, or loosely tie together a poorly conceived idea. The endorsers of said poorly conceived idea hope that: a writer will add coherence to a slapdash, weak mixture of features or non-negotiable creative details; or he/she will create yet another "thing" in a morass of endless things of which there is no vision, rigor, or organization. There's too much to do, yet not one thing of substance. And the corporate executives (aka "C-Suite") are more than aware of the product's weaknesses. Yet, they'd rather add than subtract.

"Less is more" is the conventional wisdom that is frequently ignored in this business. Therefore, what a writer needs to be vigilant of is not (just) telling a good story, but whether or not a story works for the platform at hand. And if it does, how? The "how" is very much the thrust of this book, as the previous chapters support. But the "Does it work" question... this is hardly asked because non-writers often don't understand story. They think story can be applied to anything, but it can't. They understand spectacle, they understand character, they understand world, but not the organization of information that yields a coherent journey filled with highs and lows and emotional recognition and growth of its hero. Can you deliver this creative mandate (read: genuine story; meaningful and irreplaceable content that fits organically to the platform) on, say, Alexa? Or through a VR headset? On a mobile phone experience? Or, are there some platforms where hints of it can be communicated, but not the whole megillah? Are these enough? Or are there some platforms where you just can't tell a story through it. No matter how great a writer is, one cannot ignore a gnawing truth: *A good story on an incompatible platform creates a bad experience.* Better still: *just because a certain technology can tell a story doesn't mean it should.*

A writer must then ask themselves if they want to be part of a sinking ship for pay, or if they jump ship and find an opportunity more appropriate for their craft. This is not to dissuade someone from exploring the unknown or the innovative; rather, it is to challenge them to undergird their filter for what works and what doesn't. If your story content will ultimately take the form of bells and whistles, your work is automatically not crucial to the experience; it is excisable. Sure, if you're paid on contract for a limited time frame just to create bells and whistles, then no worries. But if you expect to continue with that company indefinitely, proceed with caution. Consumers tire of bells and whistles, and they (i.e., bells and whistles) are often the first to go before a 2.0 version hits the market.

RED FLAG #5: NO VISION

No matter the size, all companies can leave themselves susceptible to setting an unclear vision. The excitement of creating a new product to fill a market need can be all-consuming and, at the same time, can create a fog. Good teams determine these market needs early on and begin the creative and engineering processes immediately thereafter with strict but achievable milestones and schedules. Bad teams, on the other hand, after falling in love with their tech's new capabilities, struggle to identify their product's primary usage or target audience and, therefore, struggle to set milestones or meet their delivery schedules.

Bad teams are far too common, unfortunately. True, they fall prey to many temptations that good teams fall to. After all, it's easy to fall in love with great tech. Innovation is exciting, especially if you created it. But good teams break from the honeymoon when the first signs of homeostasis pop up. Bad teams, on the other hand, float in it. They make infinite lateral moves and allow aimlessness to drive them.

Lack of forward momentum results from a lack of vision. A good vision – or any vision, for that matter – comprises creative north stars, target audiences, engineering milestones, financial goals, among others. A vision sets forth a shared goal which every team member works toward. The vision establishes expectations, unpacks the execution plan into achievable goals within a product cycle, and informs every part of the creative, marketing, technological, quality assurance, and financial aspect of the company. It unifies everyone, specifying everyone's roles and expectations and how they (the employees) work with others to achieve product launch.

A good vision doesn't always lead to a successful product. But a bad vision increases the likelihood of failure. And no vision at all? Well, let's put it this way:

A lackluster vision is better than no vision at all. Why? Because a lackluster vision is still a vision, and that bare minimum puts into motion the series of steps that launches a product. A team could have the greatest ideas, exuberant energy, wonderful morale, but... with constant blue sky thinking and brainstorming, analysis paralysis, love of process over execution... a team will never reach the finish line. No vision comes from deep insecurity in the team's ability and leadership, lack of discipline, and/or an aversion to setting confines and rigid milestones.

When choosing what project to work on, a writer should consider if the team has a clear product vision and a series of immutable (or nearly immutable) deadlines that escalate to launch. If a team is always kicking the can because they don't feel they're ready yet, they either failed at planning from the outset or don't know what they want or, sadly, both. It's not worth working on something new and innovative if the project will never see the light of day or if it releases at a time well past its relevance.

RED FLAG #6: FEEDING THE BEAST POORLY

Often, a new technological platform (or a content platform in general) will need content to feed its infrastructure and validate its purpose. But if the company is tech-centric, it is likely that the leadership will not have a proper gauge on: what good content is; what is required to make good content; and how the culture of content creation differs from the culture of tech. A company might look to the video game world as guidance, but with an industry that has done little to shed its pervasive, oppressive "crunch" work culture, video games fail as the proper exemplar.

Content creators – i.e., writers, content designers, interactive designers, game designers, performers – will be brought on to "feed the beast," that is, to provide as much content for the platform as possible, frequently or (preferably) relentlessly. Thanks to the internet and (on a smaller scale) the smartphone, endless content feeds customers 24 hours a day, 7 days a week. So, while the platform for which you are writing may not necessarily service those customers 24/7, expect to do so anyway. Users can binge-watch or binge-consume on multiple platforms (often concurrently) because Google Play, YouTube, Apple's iTunes, Steam, Netflix, other streaming services, and social media have set the precedent and, frankly, have shaped a culture in doing so. There is no longer such a thing as reaching the end of a VHS cassette or watching static on a TV screen come 2 a.m. Tech companies have made content – which formerly had an end – endless. As such, they transformed media into a narcotic and designed an effective syringe through its engagement mechanisms (e.g., clicks, likes, auto-play features, twitch-muscle activities on a controller or screen).

If your company doesn't have a responsible "Feed the Beast" strategy (as in, they just want as much content as possible regardless of quality), the leadership will burn out their staff and fail to determine what good content is. Yet, the Beast (aka the platform) must be fed. Consumers have adopted new habits and expectations for their technology. They want to be entertained or occupied upon nearly every waking moment. Without content that can be self-generating (like checkers or chess), a new platform cannot survive without voluminous content. Writers must expect this, must be okay with it, and must be prepared to roll up their sleeves and get to work. This is the necessary evil of this business.

The red flag isn't feeding the beast as is. Rather, it's feeding the beast with rice cakes and cotton candy. Bad content is a temptation. Quick, easy, and cheap. These are the headwinds writers confront daily.

The solution is two-fold. First, it is critical to employ a large staff of content creators, where one team works on the current content milestones; the other works on future milestones. Second, in absence of a sizable team of content creators, the company should license content from other companies or open their platform to third-party developers to create safe content for it (think Apple's App Store, Steam, or Wattpad) as an addition to its in-house content. In fact, if licensed or third-party content can align seamlessly as part of a themed slate with the platform's original content, then it's a win-win situation. I would argue, in fact, an open platform with a mixture of original, licensed, and third-party content is the vastly superior option (basically, the Netflix model). Then, original content developed by the platform team involves more manageable working hours for the staff, higher quality original content, and more time to cultivate and test said original content.

This is ideal, but it takes time and money to build those licensing and third-party partnerships. So, in the beginning months of a new platform, expect an endless need for in-house content creation. And expect the quality of the content to be, well, less than ideal. The primary goal is to prove that the platform works and can lure customer and developers. The demands to feed the beast, once again, will serve as a forcing function to accelerate the content creation process, often recklessly, often at the sacrifice of quality, often in the beginning of the platform's life cycle.

As a storyteller, you have every right to push back and demand more time and resources. Just be aware that the C-Suite is relentless in their desire for content, both in high volume and immediacy. To continue customer engagement, they will settle for (once again) fast food and rice cakes. Basically, content that is: easily digestible, low value, quick to make, superficial, quick to absorb. And lots of it. Setting the bar so low is disappointing, yet it is the reality of the industry.

The writer is most empowered when they can force evolution, so that low value content doesn't take hold for too long and cement future customer expectations of the platform. How to achieve this requires content installments released strategically over time; therefore, whatever content feeds the beast in the immediate timeline requires a corresponding set of content to be implemented in the future that is more thoughtful and meaningful. The First Wave of content is dedicated to engaging interest. The Second Wave deepens connection by increasing complexity and time worthiness. The Third Wave assures a consumer's consistent usage through emotional resonance, deeper cognitive weight, habit-forming engagement, and risk-taking with new content or new approaches to current content.

EVOLUTIONARY EXAMPLES

	First Wave	Second Wave	Third Wave
Goal	Pique interest and curiosity; find one's footing	Deepen connection by increasing complexity and time worthiness	Assure consistent usage through emotional resonance, deeper cognitive weight, and habit-forming engagement
Content Style	Brief; one-off/self-contained; similar to other experiences; easy to pick up and absorb. Or: episodically told when communicated through a medium where the audience is likely multitasking (e.g., driving while listening) and cannot devote 100% attention to the experience	Longer content or episodically told; more time with characters and world	Episodically told or a long one-off story; higher production values; longer time for story arcs; more attention on other characters; protagonist can make mistakes and not easily recover from them; taking more chances on new characters and scenarios
Content Example #1: *Insecure*	YouTube web series called *Awkward Black Girl* created by Issa Rae	*Insecure* Season #1 (TV show on HBO) – a departure from the web series, that is, different characters but similar spirit and emotional focus	*Insecure* Season #2 and onward – emotional focus involves deeper relationships and more significant fallout from mistakes
Content Example #2: *Dirty John*	A Wondery/LA Times-produced true crime podcast consisting of 6 (nearly) 40-minute episodes	A television-adapted miniseries comprising 8 (nearly) 45-minute episodes	A second season featuring different characters and a different true-to-life storyline, without a direct adaptation of the podcast. Also 8 episodes, running approximately 45 minute per episode
Content Example #3: *Destiny franchise*	A Bungie-developed first-person shooter video game filled with story missions and multiplayer collaborative missions ("strikes" or "raids"). After its 2014 release, the journey continued through downloadable expansion packs delivered annually (including *The Taken King* in 2015).	*Destiny* 2 is released in 2017 as a pay-to-play game on PS4, XboxOne, and Windows with a more robust story mode than its predecessor along with collaborative "strikes," "raids," and public event activities.	*Destiny 2: New Light* is released as a free-to-play downloadable expansion in 2019, followed by *Beyond Light* in 2020 and offers a new player experience while archiving its past campaigns such as *Curse of Osiris* and *Warmind*.

Destiny, a popular video game franchise developed by Bungie (now owned by Sony as of January 2022),[11] adopted the model of the periodic release of digital content in the way that the classic massively multiplayer online roleplaying game ("MMORPG") game *World of Warcraft* (now owned by Microsoft after its acquisition of Activision-Blizzard... also as of January 2022)[12] established as industry precedent. Once a game is released, either the story or the series of collaborative activities and events dictates a periodic update that can be downloaded through a gaming console or computer. These "expansions" (sometimes known as downloadable content or "DLC") are, sometimes, wholesale game additions. Not level or mission additions only. Think of each expansion as a completely new but related game within the franchise. These expansions can include new adventures or campaigns, often with a story that is self-contained or, at least, that extends the lore of the franchise. Because of the volume of content per each expansion, studios must schedule their expansion releases as if they were new product launches.

You'll notice that *Insecure* and *Dirty John* started out as new media on a tech platform (i.e., YouTube and iTunes podcast respectively) and moved to a traditional one (television). This typically happens when the IP, or intellectual property, outgrows its platform of origin. And while the company building a new platform is most likely not in the mindset of being outgrown, this a wonderful situation to be in as a writer. Podcasts, for example, still vie for greater awareness. A popular show on cable, like *Dirty John*, only brings greater publicity to its original medium. If you're fortunate to work for an evolving media franchise, keep in mind that adapting the story from one medium to another requires the re-envisioning of the story, either due to length and/or the modality (podcast is aural; television is visual and aural). If you do not have the skills or experience in the medium to which the IP evolves, then your role shifts from content creator to content overseer, managing the work of "hired gun" consultants who can deliver successfully within that medium.

If a company stays stagnant at the First Wave, they'll fare no better than Craig's List. That might work if you're first to market and have low overhead. But if your company is attempting to swim in the same lanes as Netflix or Steam or Apple, stagnation is your enemy.

---

[11] Pending SEC approval.
[12] Pending SEC approval.

Equally as dangerous, if the team has no concept of evolution of content, then it is critical to communicate its necessity. You must devise a content roadmap that identifies the story assets (e.g., books, comics, films, games, and/or complete episodic seasons of TV, digital series, or podcasts) that will appear within, say, the first year of launch. Each story asset should correspond to a bible or extensive write-up that includes its characters, world, story scenarios, and typical length of experience. You will also need to include the subsequent years of the content, identifying how the stories evolve and what happens to beloved characters. This roadmap allows teams to prepare appropriate budgets and assign employee resources (full-time and freelance) that can execute in the delivery of this content. The roadmap also serves as a calendar of sorts, providing an inside scoop as to what to look forward to in the immediate, intermediate, and distant futures. This forces current story content to conform to a disciplined approach in its execution. In other words, current content cannot meander and offer new story items that will run counter to future content and compromise continuity. Yes, everything is bendable, but healthy rigor creates more focused content.

RED FLAG #7: CHEMISTRY FIT... OR LACK THEREOF

Be protective of your talent. Just because a project promises to be exciting doesn't mean it will. Before hopping on board, determine whether or not you'd make a good fit for the project and team, and, just as important, whether or not they're a good fit for *you*. A lot goes into this. Team chemistry, for instance, is not something you can teach or write about; it's instinctual and doesn't materialize right away. That's why more companies offer "temp to perm" opportunities to see if either side likes working with one another before full-time employment is offered.

Take team chemistry seriously. Very seriously. If your new team will not appreciate your skills or if they ask you to do things outside of your skillset *ad infinitum*, it's likely they either do not understand what you do or they've reprioritized their product's pillars and no longer value what you've been hired to do. Neither offers a comfortable situation, but it's the latter that spells trouble. One can always clear up misunderstandings through presentations and one-on-ones so that team members know exactly what you have to offer. But if the project changed and features died along with it – namely features you were working on – leadership will question your presence. Either you (a) adapt to the new duties they require of you or (b) you don't and leave yourself vulnerable to a lay-off. This is infernally frustrating. Oftentimes, the best solution is to find a new job with another company. But if the chemistry was sound and the team is eager to keep you on in a new capacity, then you must weigh your options: (1) change to something you don't love to do but with a team that you like; or (2) find a new employer who values what you love to do while you take a gamble on the new but unknown team chemistry. Even if you were to hit it off with the new team, there's no guarantee that the synergy will continue. Employee deletions and additions leave team chemistry vulnerable. Therefore, your only weapon in the face of change is your ability to change with it.

ON THAT NOTE ...

Doom and gloom? Nope, not at all. Nor is it accurate to characterize the industry as evil, rapacious, or destructive. Yes, there are leaders who embody those traits; then again, there are leaders in every industry who do. The current state of tech needs harnessing, needs the liberal arts as well as STEM savvy. And yes – it offers vastly more good than harm. And "vastly" might be too light of an adverb.

Every part of our lives has been improved, accelerated, made more efficient, and invited more fun thanks to technology. We often complain about slow Wi-Fi today; yet 15 years ago, we connected to the internet through a phone line with constant interruptions. Or 15 years before that, we sent letters and postcards to communicate with friends in lieu of email or social media. A typical engagement is no longer weeks, but now seconds.

Technology has made surgeries more effective and less invasive in the last 30 years. Among the countless examples: Laser is used in place of a blade to correct holes in the retina. Robotic tools like the Da Vinci Surgical System offer greater precision and range of motion for colorectal, thoracis, and urologic surgeries. Less pain, faster recovery, less risk of infection – patients are the true beneficiaries of these advancements.

Entertainment, the thrust of this book, benefits too from technology, though its results vary. In the examples above, technology is the tool for healing, connecting, informing. Entertainment is not a tool, however. It is a series of experiences that provides joy, self-discovery, and excitement. It provides states of mind and, when meaningful, enrichment.

Technology dictates too heavily the quality of today's entertainment. People are engaging with numerous devices when watching a TV show on Netflix, so whoever wins the competition for the most engagement often offers the best user interface/user experience ("UI/UX"), speed, functionality, and curatorial tools. These are the elements for making a great website; yet, today, thanks to streaming services and mobile experiences, these elements apply to film, TV, games, and digital content so much so that the happy accidents of art no longer happen. This isn't to say that UI/UX, speed, functionality, and curatorial tools are mandates within a writers' room. They aren't. But the impulses behind these elements do pop in when creating, planning, and managing content.

For instance, these elements influence content acquisitions that piggyback on the styles or themes of popular shows so that they can be easily discoverable in recommendation features like "Customers Who Watched This Item Also Watched" (Amazon Prime) or "More Like This" (HBO Max). These elements also influence the modification of content for viewing on devices. The tactile UI features for interactive Netflix shows like *Black Mirror: Bandersnatch* are more successful to experience over tablet or phone than on a big screen TV where the remote control isn't as sensitive or as quickly responsive. Thus, creating a film or TV show mainly for the small screen calls for faster content (i.e., films or episodes with faster cuts, superficial storylines, light emotional investment) to compete with or to equal native mobile content. One is absorbing quickly *ala* downloading info, and lots of it. He/she is going wide, not deep. These are the new ways of media consumption, and they lead to shallow experiences.

Now, prioritizing these UI/UX elements might not seem unreasonable. Companies want to make a profit and they create different products for different customers and use whatever tools they have to figure out what those different customers want. The problem with this, though, is twofold: (1) recommendation tools aggregate data of what the most popular shows are (in general and/or by locale) at a given moment or of what a customer's completed content is. Then, the tech platforms overcompensate on that content when acquiring or developing new shows or movies. Which means there can be an oversupply of just a few genres with poor writing and production values or homogenous content. Or, if the supply is not excessive, then its discoverability through numerous recommended features is. And if its discoverability is, so too are the preferences and priorities of the corporation who owns that tech platform, especially if it has expensive licensing deals with other studios, production/publishing entities, or artists. What can result is a persistent series of "nudges" embedded with curated selection(s): "If you like horror films…", "If you like 20-something movies that take place near a lake…", "If you like movies that feature a masked villain with an axe…", "If you like movies with a character named Jason…" To which I reply: "Dear Netflix, how badly do you want me to see *Friday the 13th?????*" (2) Watching movies or films through devices undermines the intent of their original experience. Seeing images over a small screen in quick bites and in high volume equates the entertainment with a cheaply made TikTok video or a gif of a new mindless meme. It lowers the expectations of content, creates lower attention spans, and sets a lower bar of quality. Good storytelling is no longer understood when a TV show wrapped up in an app becomes redefined as just a piece of software that moves pixels around a screen.

But like Steve Jobs once said (in essence), "People don't know what they want until you give it to them." Storytellers have the power to create an innovative story experience that pushes the boundaries of tech, so that the tech serves the story and not the other way around. The current state of tech – particularly those who create it – is oblivious to quality content. This isn't to say that tech cannot produce a good story experience; rather, tech hasn't been exposed to good story on a regular basis. It is the writer's job, therefore, to advocate for the value of story and to work with designers and engineers in molding the content within the confines of the tech and demonstrating to those who want to change story for the worse why such wrong decisions will affect the user experience.

And yes, that's what it boils down to: the user experience. If the story is present in the tech just to gussy up pyrotechnics or bells and whistles, the user will see through it. If the story is muddled and incoherent because a new feature is incompatible with story, the user will see through it. If the story meanders in order to buy time for the appearance of other features or to justify them awkwardly in the user experience, the user will see through it. As mentioned earlier, focus testing will be a writer's best friend in strengthening the presence of good story and eliminating the presence of the weak. But, overall, in the absence of a testing apparatus, the end user should remain the constant focus of the content creation process. Thus, a successful marriage between content and tech begins with a few nevers: Never create for your coworkers only. Never create for your boss only. Never create for yourself only. If the culture of your team warps the focus of the product toward themselves, you've encountered the biggest red flag of them all.

REFERENCES

Online

"A Bug's Life (1998)." Box Office Mojo, https://www.boxofficemojo.com/title/tt0120623/?ref_=bo_se_r_1.

"Antz (1998)." Box Office Mojo, https://www.boxofficemojo.com/title/tt0120587/?ref_=bo_se_r_1.

"Armageddon (1998)." Box Office Mojo, https://www.boxofficemojo.com/title/tt0120591/?ref_=bo_se_r_1.

"Dante's Inferno (PS3)." VGChartz, https://www.vgchartz.com/game/32227/dantes-inferno/.

"Dante's Inferno (X360)." VGChartz, https://www.vgchartz.com/games/game.php?id=32240.

"Deep Impact (1998)." Box Office Mojo, https://www.boxofficemojo.com/title/tt0120647/?ref_=bo_se_r_1.

"God of War III (PS3)." VGChartz, https://www.vgchartz.com/game/12533/god-of-war-iii/.

Index

Printed in the United States
by Baker & Taylor Publisher Services